Children (Scotland) Act 1995

CHAPTER 36

ARRANGEMENT OF SECTIONS

PART I

PARENTS, CHILDREN AND GUARDIANS

Parental responsibilities and parental rights

PART II

PROMOTION OF CHILDREN'S WELFARE BY LOCAL AUTHORITIES AND BY CHILDREN'S HEARINGS ETC.

CHAPTER 1

SUPPORT FOR CHILDREN AND THEIR FAMILIES

Introductory

CHAPTER 2

CHILDREN'S HEARINGS

CHAPTER 3

PROTECTION AND SUPERVISION OF CHILDREN

Children requiring compulsory measures of supervision

Children (Scotland) Act 1995

1995 CHAPTER 36

An Act to reform the law of Scotland relating to children, to the adoption of children and to young persons who as children have been looked after by a local authority; to make new provision as respects the relationship between parent and child and guardian and child in the law of Scotland; to make provision as respects residential establishments for children and certain other residential establishments; and for connected purposes.

[19th July 1995]

BE IT ENACTED by the Queen's most Excellent Majesty, by and with the advice and consent of the Lords Spiritual and Temporal, and Commons, in this present Parliament assembled, and by the authority of the same, as follows:—

Part I

PARENTS, CHILDREN AND GUARDIANS

Parental responsibilities and parental rights

1.—(1) Subject to section 3(1)(b) and (3) of this Act, a parent has in relation to his child the responsibility—

   (a) to safeguard and promote the child's health, development and welfare;

   (b) to provide, in a manner appropriate to the stage of development of the child—

      (i) direction;

      (ii) guidance,

   to the child;

   (c) if the child is not living with the parent, to maintain personal relations and direct contact with the child on a regular basis; and

   (d) to act as the child's legal representative,

but only in so far as compliance with this section is practicable and in the interests of the child.

Parental responsibilities.

(2) "Child" means for the purposes of—

 (a) paragraphs (a), (b)(i), (c) and (d) of subsection (1) above, a person under the age of sixteen years;

 (b) paragraph (b)(ii) of that subsection, a person under the age of eighteen years.

(3) The responsibilities mentioned in paragraphs (a) to (d) of subsection (1) above are in this Act referred to as "parental responsibilities"; and the child, or any person acting on his behalf, shall have title to sue, or to defend, in any proceedings as respects those responsibilities.

(4) The parental responsibilities supersede any analogous duties imposed on a parent at common law; but this section is without prejudice to any other duty so imposed on him or to any duty imposed on him by, under or by virtue of any other provision of this Act or of any other enactment.

Parental rights.

2.—(1) Subject to section 3(1)(b) and (3) of this Act, a parent, in order to enable him to fulfil his parental responsibilities in relation to his child, has the right—

 (a) to have the child living with him or otherwise to regulate the child's residence;

 (b) to control, direct or guide, in a manner appropriate to the stage of development of the child, the child's upbringing;

 (c) if the child is not living with him, to maintain personal relations and direct contact with the child on a regular basis; and

 (d) to act as the child's legal representative.

(2) Subject to subsection (3) below, where two or more persons have a parental right as respects a child, each of them may exercise that right without the consent of the other or, as the case may be, of any of the others, unless any decree or deed conferring the right, or regulating its exercise, otherwise provides.

(3) Without prejudice to any court order, no person shall be entitled to remove a child habitually resident in Scotland from, or to retain any such child outwith, the United Kingdom without the consent of a person described in subsection (6) below.

(4) The rights mentioned in paragraphs (a) to (d) of subsection (1) above are in this Act referred to as "parental rights"; and a parent, or any person acting on his behalf, shall have title to sue, or to defend, in any proceedings as respects those rights.

(5) The parental rights supersede any analogous rights enjoyed by a parent at common law; but this section is without prejudice to any other right so enjoyed by him or to any right enjoyed by him by, under or by virtue of any other provision of this Act or of any other enactment.

(6) The description of a person referred to in subsection (3) above is a person (whether or not a parent of the child) who for the time being has and is exercising in relation to him a right mentioned in paragraph (a) or (c) of subsection (1) above; except that, where both the child's parents are persons so described, the consent required for his removal or retention shall be that of them both.

(7) In this section, "child" means a person under the age of sixteen years.

3.—(1) Notwithstanding section 1(1) of the Law Reform (Parent and Child) (Scotland) Act 1986 (provision for disregarding whether a person's parents are not, or have not been, married to one another in establishing the legal relationship between him and any other person)—

Provisions relating both to parental responsibilities and to parental rights.
1986 c.9.

 (a) a child's mother has parental responsibilities and parental rights in relation to him whether or not she is or has been married to his father; and

 (b) without prejudice to any arrangements which may be made under subsection (5) below and subject to any agreement which may be made under section 4 of this Act, his father has such responsibilities and rights in relation to him only if married to the mother at the time of the child's conception or subsequently.

(2) For the purposes of subsection (1)(b) above, the father shall be regarded as having been married to the mother at any time when he was a party to a purported marriage with her which was—

 (a) voidable; or

 (b) void but believed by them (whether by error of fact or of law) in good faith at that time to be valid.

(3) Subsection (1) above is without prejudice to any order made under section 11 of this Act or section 3(1) of the said Act of 1986 (provision analogous to the said section 11 but repealed by this Act) or to any other order, disposal or resolution affecting parental responsibilities or parental rights; and nothing in subsection (1) above or in this Part of this Act shall affect any other—

 (a) enactment (including any other provision of this Act or of that Act); or

 (b) rule of law,

by, under or by virtue of which a person may have imposed on him (or be relieved of) parental responsibilities or may be granted (or be deprived of) parental rights.

(4) The fact that a person has parental responsibilities or parental rights in relation to a child shall not entitle that person to act in any way which would be incompatible with any court order relating to the child or the child's property, or with any supervision requirement made under section 70 of this Act.

(5) Without prejudice to section 4(1) of this Act, a person who has parental responsibilities or parental rights in relation to a child shall not abdicate those responsibilities or rights to anyone else but may arrange for some or all of them to be fulfilled or exercised on his behalf; and without prejudice to that generality any such arrangement may be made with a person who already has parental responsibilities or parental rights in relation to the child concerned.

(6) The making of an arrangement under subsection (5) above shall not affect any liability arising from a failure to fulfil parental responsibilities; and where any arrangements so made are such that the child is a foster child for the purposes of the Foster Children (Scotland) Act 1984, those arrangements are subject to the provisions of that Act.

1984 c. 56.

Acquisition of parental rights and responsibilities by natural father.

4.—(1) Where a child's mother has not been deprived of some or all of the parental responsibilities and parental rights in relation to him and, by virtue of subsection (1)(b) of section 3 of this Act, his father has no parental responsibilities or parental rights in relation to him, the father and mother, whatever age they may be, may by agreement provide that, as from the appropriate date, the father shall have the parental responsibilities and parental rights which (in the absence of any order under section 11 of this Act affecting those responsibilities and rights) he would have if married to the mother.

(2) No agreement under subsection (1) above shall have effect unless—

    (a) in a form prescribed by the Secretary of State; and

    (b) registered in the Books of Council and Session while the mother still has the parental responsibilities and parental rights which she had when the agreement was made.

(3) The date on which such registration as is mentioned in subsection (2)(b) above takes place shall be the "appropriate date" for the purposes of subsection (1) above.

(4) An agreement which has effect by virtue of subsection (2) above shall, subject only to section 11(11) of this Act, be irrevocable.

Care or control of child by person without parental responsibilities or parental rights.

5.—(1) Subject to subsection (2) below, it shall be the responsibility of a person who has attained the age of sixteen years and who has care or control of a child under that age, but in relation to him either has no parental responsibilities or parental rights or does not have the parental responsibility mentioned in section 1(1)(a) of this Act, to do what is reasonable in all the circumstances to safeguard the child's health, development and welfare; and in fulfilling his responsibility under this section the person may in particular, even though he does not have the parental right mentioned in section 2(1)(d) of this Act, give consent to any surgical, medical or dental treatment or procedure where—

    (a) the child is not able to give such consent on his own behalf; and

    (b) it is not within the knowledge of the person that a parent of the child would refuse to give the consent in question.

(2) Nothing in this section shall apply to a person in so far as he has care or control of a child in a school ("school" having the meaning given by section 135(1) of the Education (Scotland) Act 1980).

1980 c. 44.

Views of children.

6.—(1) A person shall, in reaching any major decision which involves—

    (a) his fulfilling a parental responsibility or the responsibility mentioned in section 5(1) of this Act; or

    (b) his exercising a parental right or giving consent by virtue of that section,

have regard so far as practicable to the views (if he wishes to express them) of the child concerned, taking account of the child's age and maturity, and to those of any other person who has parental responsibilities or parental rights in relation to the child (and wishes to express those views); and without prejudice to the generality of this subsection a child twelve years of age or more shall be presumed to be of sufficient age and maturity to form a view.

(2) A transaction entered into in good faith by a third party and a person acting as legal representative of a child shall not be challengeable on the ground only that the child, or a person with parental responsibilities or parental rights in relation to the child, was not consulted or that due regard was not given to his views before the transaction was entered into.

Guardianship

7.—(1) A child's parent may appoint a person to be guardian of the child in the event of the parent's death; but—

    (a) such appointment shall be of no effect unless—

        (i) in writing and signed by the parent; and

        (ii) the parent, at the time of death, was entitled to act as legal representative of the child (or would have been so entitled if he had survived until after the birth of the child); and

    (b) any parental responsibilities or parental rights (or the right to appoint a further guardian under this section) which a surviving parent has in relation to the child shall subsist with those which, by, under or by virtue of this Part of this Act, the appointee so has.

Appointment of guardians.

(2) A guardian of a child may appoint a person to take his place as guardian in the event of the guardian's death; but such appointment shall be of no effect unless in writing and signed by the person making it.

(3) An appointment as guardian shall not take effect until accepted, either expressly or impliedly by acts which are not consistent with any other intention.

(4) If two or more persons are appointed as guardians, any one or more of them shall, unless the appointment expressly provides otherwise, be entitled to accept office even if both or all of them do not accept office.

(5) Subject to any order under section 11 or 86 of this Act, a person appointed as a child's guardian under this section shall have, in respect of the child, the responsibilities imposed, and the rights conferred, on a parent by sections 1 and 2 of this Act respectively; and sections 1 and 2 of this Act shall apply in relation to a guardian as they apply in relation to a parent.

(6) Without prejudice to the generality of subsection (1) of section 6 of this Act, a decision as to the appointment of a guardian under subsection (1) or (2) above shall be regarded for the purposes of that section (or of that section as applied by subsection (5) above) as a major decision which involves exercising a parental right.

8.—(1) An appointment made under section 7(1) or (2) of this Act revokes an earlier such appointment (including one made in an unrevoked will or codicil) made by the same person in respect of the same child, unless it is clear (whether as a result of an express provision in the later appointment or by any necessary implication) that the purpose of the later appointment is to appoint an additional guardian.

Revocation and other termination of appointment.

(2) Subject to subsections (3) and (4) below, the revocation of an appointment made under section 7(1) or (2) of this Act (including one made in an unrevoked will or codicil) shall not take effect unless the revocation is in writing and is signed by the person making the revocation.

(3) An appointment under section 7(1) or (2) of this Act (other than one made in a will or codicil) is revoked if, with the intention of revoking the appointment, the person who made it—

  (a) destroys the document by which it was made; or

  (b) has some other person destroy that document in his presence.

(4) For the avoidance of doubt, an appointment made under section 7(1) or (2) of this Act in a will or codicil is revoked if the will or codicil is revoked.

(5) Once an appointment of a guardian has taken effect under section 7 of this Act, then, unless the terms of the appointment provide for earlier termination, it shall terminate only by virtue of—

  (a) the child concerned attaining the age of eighteen years;

  (b) the death of the child or the guardian; or

  (c) the termination of the appointment by a court order under section 11 of this Act.

Administration of child's property

Safeguarding of
child's property.

9.—(1) Subject to section 13 of this Act, this section applies where—

  (a) property is owned by or due to a child;

  (b) the property is held by a person other than a parent or guardian of the child; and

  (c) but for this section, the property would be required to be transferred to a parent having parental responsibilities in relation to the child or to a guardian for administration by that parent or guardian on behalf of the child.

(2) Subject to subsection (4) below, where this section applies and the person holding the property is an executor or trustee, then—

  (a) if the value of the property exceeds £20,000, he shall; or

  (b) if that value is not less than £5,000 and does not exceed £20,000, he may,

apply to the Accountant of Court for a direction as to the administration of the property.

(3) Subject to subsection (4) below, where this section applies and the person holding the property is a person other than an executor or trustee, then, if the value of the property is not less than £5,000, that person may apply to the Accountant of Court for a direction as to the administration of the property.

(4) Where the parent or guardian mentioned in subsection (1)(c) above has been appointed a trustee under a trust deed to administer the property concerned, subsections (2) and (3) above shall not apply, and the person holding the property shall transfer it to the parent or guardian.

(5) On receipt of an application under subsection (2) or (3) above, the Accountant of Court may do one, or (in so far as the context admits) more than one, of the following—

(a) apply to the court for the appointment of a judicial factor (whether or not the parent or guardian mentioned in subsection (1)(c) above) to administer all or part of the property concerned and in the event of the court making such an appointment shall direct that the property, or as the case may be part, concerned be transferred to the factor;

(b) direct that all or part of the property concerned be transferred to himself;

(c) direct that all or, in a case where the parent or guardian so mentioned has not been appointed by virtue of paragraph (a) above, part of the property concerned be transferred to the parent or guardian,

to be administered on behalf of the child.

(6) A direction under subsection (5)(c) above may include such conditions as the Accountant of Court considers appropriate, including in particular a condition—

(a) that in relation to the property concerned no capital expenditure shall be incurred without his approval; or

(b) that there shall be exhibited annually to him the securities and bank books which represent the capital of the estate.

(7) A person who has applied under subsection (2) or (3) above for a direction shall not thereafter transfer the property concerned except in accordance with a direction under subsection (5) above.

(8) The Secretary of State may from time to time prescribe a variation in any sum referred to in subsections (2) and (3) above.

(9) In this section "child" means a person under the age of sixteen years who is habitually resident in Scotland.

10.—(1) A person acting as a child's legal representative in relation to the administration of the child's property—

(a) shall be required to act as a reasonable and prudent person would act on his own behalf; and

(b) subject to any order made under section 11 of this Act, shall be entitled to do anything which the child, if of full age and capacity, could do in relation to that property;

and subject to subsection (2) below, on ceasing to act as legal representative, shall be liable to account to the child for his intromissions with the child's property.

Obligations and rights of person administering child's property.

(2) No liability shall be incurred by virtue of subsection (1) above in respect of funds which have been used in the proper discharge of the person's responsibility to safeguard and promote the child's health, development and welfare.

Court Orders

11.—(1) In the relevant circumstances in proceedings in the Court of Session or sheriff court, whether those proceedings are or are not independent of any other action, an order may be made under this subsection in relation to—

(a) parental responsibilities;

Court orders relating to parental responsibilities etc.

(b) parental rights;

(c) guardianship; or

(d) subject to section 14(1) and (2) of this Act, the administration of a child's property.

(2) The court may make such order under subsection (1) above as it thinks fit; and without prejudice to the generality of that subsection may in particular so make any of the following orders—

(a) an order depriving a person of some or all of his parental responsibilities or parental rights in relation to a child;

(b) an order—

(i) imposing upon a person (provided he is at least sixteen years of age or is a parent of the child) such responsibilities; and

(ii) giving that person such rights;

(c) an order regulating the arrangements as to—

(i) with whom; or

(ii) if with different persons alternately or periodically, with whom during what periods,

a child under the age of sixteen years is to live (any such order being known as a "residence order");

(d) an order regulating the arrangements for maintaining personal relations and direct contact between a child under that age and a person with whom the child is not, or will not be, living (any such order being known as a "contact order");

(e) an order regulating any specific question which has arisen, or may arise, in connection with any of the matters mentioned in paragraphs (a) to (d) of subsection (1) of this section (any such order being known as a "specific issue order") ;

(f) an interdict prohibiting the taking of any step of a kind specified in the interdict in the fulfillment of parental responsibilities or the exercise of parental rights relating to a child or in the administration of a child's property;

(g) an order appointing a judicial factor to manage a child's property or remitting the matter to the Accountant of Court to report on suitable arrangements for the future management of the property; or

(h) an order appointing or removing a person as guardian of the child.

(3) The relevant circumstances mentioned in subsection (1) above are—

(a) that application for an order under that subsection is made by a person who—

(i) not having, and never having had, parental responsibilities or parental rights in relation to the child, claims an interest;

(ii) has parental responsibilities or parental rights in relation to the child;

(iii) has had, but for a reason other than is mentioned in subsection (4) below no longer has, parental responsibilities or parental rights in relation to the child; or

(b) that although no such application has been made, the court (even if it declines to make any other order) considers it should make such an order.

(4) The reasons referred to in subsection (3)(a)(iii) above are that the parental responsibilities or parental rights have been—

(a) extinguished on the making of an adoption order;

(b) transferred to an adoption agency on the making of an order declaring the child free for adoption;

(c) extinguished by virtue of subsection (9) of section 30 of the Human Fertilisation and Embryology Act 1990 (provision for enactments about adoption to have effect with modifications) on the making of a parental order under subsection (1) of that section; or

1990 c. 37.

(d) transferred to a local authority by a parental responsibilities order.

(5) In subsection (3)(a) above "person" includes (without prejudice to the generality of that subsection) the child concerned; but it does not include a local authority.

(6) In subsection (4) above—

"adoption agency" and "adoption order" have the same meanings as they are given, in section 18 of the Adoption (Scotland) Act 1978, by section 65(1) of that Act; and

1978 c. 28.

"parental responsibilities order" has the meaning given by section 86(1) of this Act.

(7) Subject to subsection (8) below, in considering whether or not to make an order under subsection (1) above and what order to make, the court—

(a) shall regard the welfare of the child concerned as its paramount consideration and shall not make any such order unless it considers that it would be better for the child that the order be made than that none should be made at all; and

(b) taking account of the child's age and maturity, shall so far as practicable—

(i) give him an opportunity to indicate whether he wishes to express his views;

(ii) if he does so wish, give him an opportunity to express them; and

(iii) have regard to such views as he may express.

(8) The court shall, notwithstanding subsection (7) above, endeavour to ensure that any order which it makes, or any determination by it not to make an order, does not adversely affect the position of a person who has, in good faith and for value, acquired any property of the child concerned, or any right or interest in such property.

(9) Nothing in paragraph (b) of subsection (7) above requires a child to be legally represented, if he does not wish to be, in proceedings in the course of which the court implements that paragraph.

(10) Without prejudice to the generality of paragraph (b) of subsection (7) above, a child twelve years of age or more shall be presumed to be of sufficient age and maturity to form a view for the purposes both of that paragraph and of subsection (9) above.

(11) An order under subsection (1) above shall have the effect of depriving a person of a parental responsibility or parental right only in so far as the order expressly so provides and only to the extent necessary to give effect to the order; but in making any such order as is mentioned in paragraph (a) or (b) of subsection (2) above the court may revoke any agreement which, in relation to the child concerned, has effect by virtue of section 4(2) of this Act.

(12) Where the court makes a residence order which requires that a child live with a person who, immediately before the order is made does not have in relation to the child all the parental responsibilities mentioned in paragraphs (a), (b) and (d) of section 1(1), and the parental rights mentioned in paragraphs (b) and (d) of section 2(1), of this Act (those which he does not so have being in this subsection referred to as the "relevant responsibilities and rights") that person shall, subject to the provisions of the order or of any other order made under subsection (1) above, have the relevant responsibilities and rights while the residence order remains in force.

(13) Any reference in this section to an order includes a reference to an interim order or to an order varying or discharging an order.

Restrictions on decrees for divorce, separation or annulment affecting children.

12.—(1) In any action for divorce, judicial separation or declarator of nullity of marriage, the court shall, where this section applies, consider (in the light of such information as is before the court as to the arrangements which have been, or are proposed to be, made for the upbringing of each child by virtue of which it applies) whether to exercise with respect to him the powers conferred by section 11 or 54 of this Act.

(2) Where, in any case to which this section applies, the court is of the opinion that—

    (a) the circumstances of the case require, or are likely to require, it to exercise any power under section 11 or 54 of this Act with respect to the child concerned;

    (b) it is not in a position to exercise that power without giving further consideration to the case; and

    (c) there are exceptional circumstances which make it desirable in the interests of that child that it should not grant decree in the action until it is in a position to exercise such a power,

it shall postpone its decision on the granting of decree in the action until it is in such a position.

(3) This section applies where a child of the family has not reached the age of sixteen years at the date when the question first arises as to whether the court should give such consideration as is mentioned in subsection (1) above.

(4) In this section "child of the family", in relation to the parties to a marriage, means—

    (a) a child of both of them; or

(b) any other child, not being a child who is placed with them as foster parents by a local authority or voluntary organisation, who has been treated by both of them as a child of their family.

13.—(1) Where in any court proceedings a sum of money becomes payable to, or for the benefit of, a child under the age of sixteen years, the court may make such order relating to the payment and management of the sum for the benefit of the child as it thinks fit.

(2) Without prejudice to the generality of subsection (1) above, the court may in an order under this section—

(a) appoint a judicial factor to invest, apply or otherwise deal with the money for the benefit of the child concerned;

(b) order the money to be paid—

(i) to the sheriff clerk or the Accountant of Court; or

(ii) to a parent or guardian of that child,

to be invested, applied or otherwise dealt with, under the directions of the court, for the benefit of that child; or

(c) order the money to be paid directly to that child.

(3) Where payment is made to a person in accordance with an order under this section, a receipt given by him shall be a sufficient discharge of the obligation to make the payment.

Jurisdiction and choice of law

14.—(1) The Court of Session shall have jurisdiction to entertain an application for an order relating to the administration of a child's property if the child is habitually resident in, or the property is situated in, Scotland.

(2) A sheriff shall have jurisdiction to entertain such an application if the child is habitually resident in, or the property is situated in, the sheriffdom.

(3) Subject to subsection (4) below, any question arising under this Part of this Act—

(a) concerning—

(i) parental responsibilities or parental rights; or

(ii) the responsibilities or rights of a guardian,

in relation to a child shall, in so far as it is not also a question such as is mentioned in paragraph (b) below, be determined by the law of the place of the child's habitual residence at the time when the question arises;

(b) concerning the immediate protection of a child shall be determined by the law of the place where the child is when the question arises; and

(c) as to whether a person is validly appointed or constituted guardian of a child shall be determined by the law of the place of the child's habitual residence on the date when the appointment was made (the date of death of the testator being taken to be the date of appointment where an appointment was made by will), or the event constituting the guardianship occurred.

(4) Nothing in any provision of law in accordance with which, under subsection (3) above, a question which arises in relation to an application for, or the making of, an order under subsection (1) of section 11 of this Act falls to be determined, shall affect the application of subsection (7) of that section.

Interpretation

Interpretation of Part I.

15.—(1) In this Part of this Act—

"child" means, where the expression is not otherwise defined, a person under the age of eighteen years;

"contact order" has the meaning given by section 11(2)(d) of this Act;

1978 c.28.
1990 c.37.

"parent", in relation to any person, means, subject to Part IV of the Adoption (Scotland) Act 1978 and sections 27 to 30 of the Human Fertilisation and Embryology Act 1990 and any regulations made under subsection (9) of the said section 30, someone, of whatever age, who is that person's genetic father or mother;

"parental responsibilities" has the meaning given by section 1(3) of this Act;

"parental rights" has the meaning given by section 2(4) of this Act;

"residence order" has the meaning given by section 11(2)(c) of this Act;

"specific issue order" has the meaning given by section 11(2)(e) of this Act; and

1991 c.50.

"transaction" has the meaning given by section 9 of the Age of Legal Capacity (Scotland) Act 1991 (except that, for the purposes of subsection (5)(b) below, paragraph (d) of the definition in question shall be disregarded).

(2) No provision in this Part of this Act shall affect any legal proceedings commenced, or any application made to a court, before that provision comes into effect; except that where, before section 11 of this Act comes into force, there has been final decree in a cause in which, as respects a child, an order for custody or access, or an order which is analogous to any such order as is mentioned in subsection (2) of that section, has been made, any application on or after the date on which the section does come into force for variation or recall of the order shall proceed as if the order had been made under that section.

(3) In subsection (2) above, the reference to final decree is to a decree or interlocutor which, taken by itself or along with previous interlocutors, disposes of the whole subject matter of the cause.

(4) Any reference in this Part of this Act to a person—

(a) having parental rights or responsibilities;

(b) acting as a legal representative; or

(c) being appointed a guardian,

is to a natural person only.

(5) Any reference in this Part of this Act to a person acting as the legal representative of a child is a reference to that person, in the interests of the child—

(a) administering any property belonging to the child; and

(b) acting in, or giving consent to, any transaction where the child is incapable of so acting or consenting on his own behalf.

(6) Where a child has legal capacity to sue, or to defend, in any civil proceedings, he may nevertheless consent to be represented in those proceedings by any person who, had the child lacked that capacity, would have had the responsibility to act as his legal representative.

Part II

PROMOTION OF CHILDREN'S WELFARE BY LOCAL AUTHORITIES AND BY CHILDREN'S HEARINGS ETC.

CHAPTER 1

SUPPORT FOR CHILDREN AND THEIR FAMILIES

Introductory

16.—(1) Where under or by virtue of this Part of this Act, a children's hearing decide, or a court determines, any matter with respect to a child the welfare of that child throughout his childhood shall be their or its paramount consideration.

Welfare of child and consideration of his views.

(2) In the circumstances mentioned in subsection (4) below, a children's hearing or as the case may be the sheriff, taking account of the age and maturity of the child concerned, shall so far as practicable—

(a) give him an opportunity to indicate whether he wishes to express his views;

(b) if he does so wish, give him an opportunity to express them; and

(c) have regard to such views as he may express;

and without prejudice to the generality of this subsection a child twelve years of age or more shall be presumed to be of sufficient age and maturity to form a view.

(3) In the circumstances mentioned in subsection (4)(a)(i) or (ii) or (b) of this section, no requirement or order so mentioned shall be made with respect to the child concerned unless the children's hearing consider, or as the case may be the sheriff considers, that it would be better for the child that the requirement or order be made than that none should be made at all.

(4) The circumstances to which subsection (2) above refers are that—

(a) the children's hearing—

    (i) are considering whether to make, or are reviewing, a supervision requirement;

    (ii) are considering whether to grant a warrant under subsection (1) of section 66, or subsection (4) or (7) of section 69, of this Act or to provide under subsection (5) of the said section 66 for the continuation of a warrant;

    (iii) are engaged in providing advice under section 60(10) of this Act; or

    (iv) are drawing up a report under section 73(13) of this Act;

(b) the sheriff is considering—

(i) whether to make, vary or discharge a parental responsibilities order, a child assessment order or an exclusion order;

(ii) whether to vary or discharge a child protection order;

(iii) whether to grant a warrant under section 67 of this Act; or

(iv) on appeal, whether to make such substitution as is mentioned in section 51(5)(c)(iii) of this Act; or

(c) the sheriff is otherwise disposing of an appeal against a decision of a children's hearing.

(5) If, for the purpose of protecting members of the public from serious harm (whether or not physical harm)—

(a) a children's hearing consider it necessary to make a decision under or by virtue of this Part of this Act which (but for this paragraph) would not be consistent with their affording paramountcy to the consideration mentioned in subsection (1) above, they may make that decision; or

(b) a court considers it necessary to make a determination under or by virtue of Chapters 1 to 3 of this Part of this Act which (but for this paragraph) would not be consistent with its affording such paramountcy, it may make that determination.

Duty of local authority to child looked after by them.

17.—(1) Where a child is looked after by a local authority they shall, in such manner as the Secretary of State may prescribe—

(a) safeguard and promote his welfare (which shall, in the exercise of their duty to him be their paramount concern);

(b) make such use of services available for children cared for by their own parents as appear to the authority reasonable in his case; and

(c) take such steps to promote, on a regular basis, personal relations and direct contact between the child and any person with parental responsibilities in relation to him as appear to them to be, having regard to their duty to him under paragraph (a) above, both practicable and appropriate.

(2) The duty under paragraph (a) of subsection (1) above includes, without prejudice to that paragraph's generality, the duty of providing advice and assistance with a view to preparing the child for when he is no longer looked after by a local authority.

(3) Before making any decision with respect to a child whom they are looking after, or proposing to look after, a local authority shall, so far as is reasonably practicable, ascertain the views of—

(a) the child;

(b) his parents;

(c) any person who is not a parent of his but who has parental rights in relation to him; and

(d) any other person whose views the authority consider to be relevant,

regarding the matter to be decided.

(4) In making any such decision a local authority shall have regard so far as practicable—

  (a) to the views (if he wishes to express them) of the child concerned, taking account of his age and maturity;

  (b) to such views of any person mentioned in subsection (3)(b) to (d) above as they have been able to ascertain; and

  (c) to the child's religious persuasion, racial origin and cultural and linguistic background.

(5) If, for the purpose of protecting members of the public from serious harm (whether or not physical harm) a local authority consider it necessary to exercise, in a manner which (but for this paragraph) would not be consistent with their duties under this section, their powers with respect to a child whom they are looking after, they may do so.

(6) Any reference in this Chapter of this Part to a child who is "looked after" by a local authority, is to a child—

  (a) for whom they are providing accommodation under section 25 of this Act;

  (b) who is subject to a supervision requirement and in respect of whom they are the relevant local authority;

  (c) who is subject to an order made, or authorisation or warrant granted, by virtue of Chapter 2, 3 or 4 of this Part of this Act, being an order, authorisation or warrant in accordance with which they have responsibilities as respects the child; or

  (d) who is subject to an order in accordance with which, by virtue of regulations made under section 33(1) of this Act, they have such responsibilities.

(7) Regulations made by the Secretary of State under subsection (1) above may, without prejudice to the generality of that subsection, include—

  (a) provision as to the circumstances in which the child may be cared for by the child's own parents; and

  (b) procedures which shall be followed in the event of the child's death.

18.—(1) Where a child is being looked after by a local authority, each natural person who has parental responsibilities in relation to the child shall, without unreasonable delay, inform that authority whenever the person changes his address.

Duty of persons with parental responsibilities to notify change of address to local authority looking after child.

(2) A person who knowingly fails to comply with the requirement imposed by subsection (1) above shall be liable on summary conviction to a fine of level 1 on the standard scale; but in any proceedings under this section it shall be a defence that—

  (a) the change was to the same address as that to which another person who at that time had parental responsibilities in relation to the child was changing; and

  (b) the accused had reasonable cause to believe that the other person had informed the authority of the change of address of them both.

Local authority
plans for services
for children.

Provision of services

19.—(1) Within such period after the coming into force of this section as the Secretary of State may direct, each local authority shall prepare and publish a plan for the provision of relevant services for or in respect of children in their area.

(2) References to "relevant services" in this section are to services provided by a local authority under or by virtue of—

(a) this Part of this Act; or

1968 c. 49.

(b) any of the enactments mentioned in section 5(1B)(a) to (o) of the Social Work (Scotland) Act 1968 (enactments in respect of which Secretary of State may issue directions to local authorities as to the exercise of their functions).

(3) A local authority shall from time to time review the plan prepared by them under subsection (1) above (as modified, or last substituted, under this subsection) and may, having regard to that review, prepare and publish—

(a) modifications (or as the case may be further modifications) to the plan reviewed; or

(b) a plan in substitution for that plan.

(4) The Secretary of State may, subject to subsection (5) below, issue directions as to the carrying out by a local authority of their functions under subsection (3) above.

(5) In preparing any plan, or carrying out any review, under this section a local authority shall consult—

1978 c. 29.

(a) every Health Board and National Health Service trust providing services under the National Health Service (Scotland) Act 1978 in the area of the authority;

(b) such voluntary organisations as appear to the authority—

(i) to represent the interests of persons who use or are likely to use relevant services in that area; or

(ii) to provide services in that area which, were they to be provided by the authority, might be categorised as relevant services;

1994 c.39.

(c) the Principal Reporter appointed under section 127 of the Local Government etc. (Scotland) Act 1994;

(d) the chairman of the children's panel for that area;

(e) such housing associations, voluntary housing agencies and other bodies as appear to the authority to provide housing in that area; and

(f) such other persons as the Secretary of State may direct.

Publication of
information about
services for
children.

20.—(1) A local authority shall, within such period after the coming into force of this section as the Secretary of State may direct, and thereafter from time to time, prepare and publish information—

(a) about relevant services which are provided by them for or in respect of children (including, without prejudice to that generality, services for or in respect of disabled children or children otherwise affected by disability) in their area or by any other local authority for those children; and

(b) where they consider it appropriate, about services which are provided by voluntary organisations and by other persons for those children, being services which the authority have power to provide and which, were they to do so, they would provide as relevant services.

(2) In subsection (1) above, "relevant services" has the same meaning as in section 19 of this Act.

21.—(1) Where it appears to a local authority that an appropriate person could, by doing certain things, help in the exercise of any of their functions under this Part of this Act, they may, specifying what those things are, request the help of that person.

Co-operation between authorities.

(2) For the purposes of subsection (1) above, persons who are appropriate are—

(a) any other local authority;

(b) a health board constituted under section 2 of the National Health Service (Scotland) Act 1978;

1978 c. 29.

(c) a national health service trust established under section 12A of that Act; and

(d) any person authorised by the Secretary of State for the purposes of this section;

and an appropriate person receiving such a request shall comply with it provided that it is compatible with their own statutory or other duties and obligations and (in the case of a person not a natural person) does not unduly prejudice the discharge of any of their functions.

22.—(1) A local authority shall—

(a) safeguard and promote the welfare of children in their area who are in need; and

Promotion of welfare of children in need.

(b) so far as is consistent with that duty, promote the upbringing of such children by their families,

by providing a range and level of services appropriate to the children's needs.

(2) In providing services under subsection (1) above, a local authority shall have regard so far as practicable to each child's religious persuasion, racial origin and cultural and linguistic background.

(3) Without prejudice to the generality of subsection (1) above—

(a) a service may be provided under that subsection—

(i) for a particular child;

(ii) if provided with a view to safeguarding or promoting his welfare, for his family; or

(iii) if provided with such a view, for any other member of his family; and

(b) the services mentioned in that subsection may include giving assistance in kind or, in exceptional circumstances, in cash.

(4) Assistance such as is mentioned in subsection (3)(b) above may be given unconditionally or subject to conditions as to the repayment, in whole or in part, of it or of its value; but before giving it, or imposing such

PART II

conditions, the local authority shall have regard to the means of the child concerned and of his parents and no condition shall require repayment by a person at any time when in receipt of—

1992 c.4.

(a) income support or family credit payable under the Social Security Contributions and Benefits Act 1992; or

1995 c. 18.

(b) an income-based jobseeker's allowance payable under the Jobseekers Act 1995.

Children affected by disability.

23.—(1) Without prejudice to the generality of subsection (1) of section 22 of this Act, services provided by a local authority under that subsection shall be designed—

(a) to minimise the effect on any—

(i) disabled child who is within the authority's area, of his disability; and

(ii) child who is within that area and is affected adversely by the disability of any other person in his family, of that other person's disability; and

(b) to give those children the opportunity to lead lives which are as normal as possible.

(2) For the purposes of this Chapter of this Part a person is disabled if he is chronically sick or disabled or suffers from mental disorder (within the meaning of the Mental Health (Scotland) Act 1984).

1984 c.36.

(3) Where requested to do so by a child's parent or guardian a local authority shall, for the purpose of facilitating the discharge of such duties as the authority may have under section 22(1) of this Act (whether or not by virtue of subsection (1) above) as respects the child, carry out an assessment of the child, or of any other person in the child's family, to determine the needs of the child in so far as attributable to his disability or to that of the other person.

Assessment of ability of carers to provide care for disabled children.

24.—(1) Subject to subsection (2) below, in any case where—

(a) a local authority carry out under section 23(3) of this Act an assessment to determine the needs of a disabled child, and

(b) a person (in this section referred to as the "carer") provides or intends to provide a substantial amount of care on a regular basis for that child,

the carer may request the local authority, before they make a decision as to the discharge of any duty they may have under section 2(1) of the Chronically Sick and Disabled Persons Act 1970 or under section 22(1) of this Act as respects the child, to carry out an assessment of the carer's ability to continue to provide, or as the case may be to provide, care for that child; and if the carer makes such a request, the local authority shall carry out such an assessment and shall have regard to the results of it in making any such decision.

1970 c.44.

(2) No request may be made under subsection (1) above by a person who provides or will provide the care in question—

(a) under or by virtue of a contract of employment or other contract; or

(b) as a volunteer for a voluntary organisation.

(3) Where an assessment of a carer's ability to continue to provide, or as the case may be to provide, care for a child is carried out under subsection (1) above, there shall, as respects the child, be no requirement under section 8 of the Disabled Persons (Services, Consultation and Representation) Act 1986 (carer's ability to continue to provide care to be considered in any decision as respects provision of certain services for disabled persons) to have regard to that ability.

(4) In this section "person" means a natural person.

25.—(1) A local authority shall provide accommodation for any child who, residing or having been found within their area, appears to them to require such provision because—

    (a) no-one has parental responsibility for him;

    (b) he is lost or abandoned; or

    (c) the person who has been caring for him is prevented, whether or not permanently and for whatever reason, from providing him with suitable accommodation or care.

(2) Without prejudice to subsection (1) above, a local authority may provide accommodation for any child within their area if they consider that to do so would safeguard or promote his welfare.

(3) A local authority may provide accommodation for any person within their area who is at least eighteen years of age but not yet twenty-one, if they consider that to do so would safeguard or promote his welfare.

(4) A local authority providing accommodation under subsection (1) above for a child who is ordinarily resident in the area of another local authority shall notify the other authority, in writing, that such provision is being made; and the other authority may at any time take over the provision of accommodation for the child.

(5) Before providing a child with accommodation under this section, a local authority shall have regard, so far as practicable, to his views (if he wishes to express them), taking account of his age and maturity; and without prejudice to the generality of this subsection a child twelve years of age or more shall be presumed to be of sufficient age and maturity to form a view.

(6) Subject to subsection (7) below—

    (a) a local authority shall not provide accommodation under this section for a child if any person who—

        (i) has parental responsibilities in relation to him and the parental rights mentioned in section 2(1)(a) and (b) of this Act; and

        (ii) is willing and able either to provide, or to arrange to have provided, accommodation for him,

    objects; and

    (b) any such person may at any time remove the child from accommodation which has been provided by the local authority under this section.

(7) Paragraph (a) of subsection (6) above does not apply—

(a) as respects any child who, being at least sixteen years of age, agrees to be provided with accommodation under this section; or

(b) where a residence order has been made in favour of one or more persons and that person has, or as the case may be those persons have, agreed that the child should be looked after in accommodation provided by, or on behalf of, the local authority;

and paragraph (b) of that subsection does not apply where accommodation has been provided for a continuous period of at least six months (whether by a single local authority or, by virtue of subsection (4) above, by more than one local authority), unless the person removing the child has given the local authority for the time being making such provision at least fourteen days' notice in writing of his intention to remove the child.

(8) In this Part of this Act, accommodation means, except where the context otherwise requires, accommodation provided for a continuous period of more than twenty-four hours.

Manner of provision of accommodation to child looked after by local authority.

26.—(1) A local authority may provide accommodation for a child looked after by them by—

(a) placing him with—

(i) a family (other than such family as is mentioned in paragraph (a) or (b) of the definition of that expression in section 93(1) of this Act);

(ii) a relative of his; or

(iii) any other suitable person,

on such terms as to payment, by the authority or otherwise, as the authority may determine;

(b) maintaining him in a residential establishment; or

(c) making such other arrangements as appear to them to be appropriate, including (without prejudice to the generality of this paragraph) making use of such services as are referred to in section 17(1)(b) of this Act.

(2) A local authority may arrange for a child whom they are looking after—

(a) to be placed, under subsection (1)(a) above, with a person in England and Wales or in Northern Ireland; or

(b) to be maintained in any accommodation in which—

1989 c.41.

(i) a local authority in England and Wales could maintain him by virtue of section 23(2)(b) to (e) of the Children Act 1989; or

S.I. 1995/755 (N.I.2)

(ii) an authority within the meaning of the Children (Northern Ireland) Order 1995 could maintain him by virtue of Article 27(2)(b) to (e) of that Order.

Day care for pre-school and other children.

27.—(1) Each local authority shall provide such day care for children in need within their area who—

(a) are aged five or under; and

(b) have not yet commenced attendance at a school,

as is appropriate; and they may provide such day care for children within their area who satisfy the conditions mentioned in paragraphs (a) and (b) but are not in need.

(2) A local authority may provide facilities (including training, advice, guidance and counselling) for those—

(a) caring for children in day care; or

(b) who at any time accompany such children while they are in day care.

(3) Each local authority shall provide for children in need within their area who are in attendance at a school such care—

(a) outside school hours; or

(b) during school holidays,

as is appropriate; and they may provide such care for children within their area who are in such attendance but are not in need.

(4) In this section—

"day care" means any form of care provided for children during the day, whether or not it is provided on a regular basis; and

"school" has the meaning given by section 135(1) of the Education (Scotland) Act 1980.

1980 c. 44.

28. Section 23 of the Social Work (Scotland) Act 1968 (which provides a power for local authorities and voluntary associations, with the consent of the Secretary of State, to make arrangements for the emigration of children in their care) shall cease to have effect.

Removal of power to arrange for emigration of children.

1968 c.49.

Advice and assistance for young persons formerly looked after by local authorities

29.—(1) A local authority shall, unless they are satisfied that his welfare does not require it, advise, guide and assist any person in their area over school age but not yet nineteen years of age who, at the time when he ceased to be of school age or at any subsequent time was, but who is no longer, looked after by a local authority.

After-care.

(2) If a person within the area of a local authority is at least nineteen, but is less than twenty-one, years of age and is otherwise a person such as is described in subsection (1) above, he may by application to the authority request that they provide him with advice, guidance and assistance; and they may, unless they are satisfied that his welfare does not require it, grant that application.

(3) Assistance given under subsection (1) or (2) above may include assistance in kind or in cash.

(4) Where a person—

(a) over school age ceases to be looked after by a local authority; or

(b) described in subsection (1) above is being provided with advice, guidance or assistance by a local authority,

they shall, if he proposes to reside in the area of another local authority, inform that other local authority accordingly provided that he consents to their doing so.

PART II
Financial
assistance towards
expenses of
education or
training and
removal of power
to guarantee
indentures etc.
1968 c. 49.

30.—(1) Without prejudice to section 12 of the Social Work (Scotland) Act 1968 (general social welfare services of local authorities), a local authority may make—

(a) grants to any relevant person in their area to enable him to meet expenses connected with his receiving education or training; and

(b) contributions to the accommodation and maintenance of any such person in any place near where he may be—

(i) employed, or seeking employment; or

(ii) receiving education or training.

(2) Subject to subsection (3) below, a person is a relevant person for the purposes of subsection (1) above if—

(a) he is over school age but not yet twenty-one years of age; and

(b) at the time when he ceased to be of school age or at any subsequent time he was, but he is no longer, looked after by a local authority.

(3) A local authority making grants under paragraph (a), or contributions under paragraph (b)(ii), of subsection (1) above to a person may continue to make them, though he has in the meantime attained the age of twenty-one years, until he completes the course of education or training in question; but if, after he has attained that age, the course is interrupted by any circumstances they may only so continue if he resumes the course as soon as is practicable.

(4) Section 25 of the Social Work (Scotland) Act 1968 (which empowers a local authority to undertake obligations by way of guarantee under any indentures or other deed of apprenticeship or articles of clerkship entered into by a person in their care or under supplemental deeds or articles) shall cease to have effect.

Miscellaneous and General

Review of case of
child looked after
by local authority.

31.—(1) Without prejudice to their duty under section 17(1)(a) of this Act, it shall be the duty of a local authority who are looking after a child to review his case at such intervals as may be prescribed by the Secretary of State.

(2) The Secretary of State may prescribe—

(a) different intervals in respect of the first such review and in respect of subsequent reviews;

(b) the manner in which cases are to be reviewed under this section;

(c) the considerations to which the local authority are to have regard in reviewing cases under this section.

32. A local authority, notwithstanding any agreement made in connection with the placing of a child in a residential establishment under this Chapter, or Chapter 4, of this Part of this Act by them—

(a) may, at any time; and

(b) shall, if requested to do so by the person responsible for the establishment,

remove a child so placed.

PART II

Effect of orders
etc. made in
different parts of
the United
Kingdom.

33.—(1) The Secretary of State may make regulations providing for a prescribed order which is made by a court in England and Wales or in Northern Ireland, if that order appears to him to correspond generally to an order of a kind which may be made under this Part of this Act or to a supervision requirement, to have effect in prescribed circumstances and for prescribed purposes of the law of Scotland as if it were an order of that kind or, as the case may be, as if it were a supervision requirement.

(2) The Secretary of State may make regulations providing—

    (a) for a prescribed order made under this Part of this Act by a court in Scotland; or

    (b) for a supervision requirement,

if that order or requirement appears to him to correspond generally to an order of a kind which may be made under any provision of law in force in England and Wales or in Northern Ireland, to have effect in prescribed circumstances and for prescribed purposes of the law of England and Wales, or as the case may be of Northern Ireland, as if it were an order of that kind.

(3) Regulations under subsection (1) or (2)(a) above may provide for the order given effect for prescribed purposes to cease to have effect for those purposes, or for the purposes of the law of the place where the order was made, if prescribed conditions are satisfied.

(4) Where a child who is subject to a supervision requirement is lawfully taken to live in England and Wales or in Northern Ireland, the requirement shall cease to have effect if prescribed conditions are satisfied.

(5) Regulations under this section may modify any provision of—

    (a) the Social Work (Scotland) Act 1968 or this Act in any application which the Acts may respectively have, by virtue of the regulations, in relation to an order made otherwise than in Scotland;   1968 c. 49.

    (b) the Children Act 1989 or the Children and Young Persons Act 1969 in any application which those Acts may respectively have, by virtue of the regulations, in relation to an order prescribed under subsection (2)(a) above or to a supervision requirement; or   1989 c. 41.
1969 c. 54.

    (c) the Children (Northern Ireland) Order 1995 or the Children and Young Persons Act (Northern Ireland) 1968 in any application which they may respectively have, by virtue of the regulations, in relation to an order so prescribed or to a supervision requirement.   S.I. 1995/755 (N.I.2)
1968 c. 34 (N.I.)

34.—(1) Part IV of the Social Work (Scotland) Act 1968 (which makes provision as regards residential and other establishments) shall be amended in accordance with this section.   Registration and inspection of certain residential grant-aided and independent schools etc.

(2) In section 61 (restriction on carrying on of establishments)—

    (a) for subsection (1) there shall be substituted—

"(1) In so far as the context admits, the following provisions of this Part of this Act apply—

(a) except in the case mentioned in paragraph (b) below, to any residential or other establishment the whole or a substantial part of whose functions is to provide persons with such personal care or support, whether or not combined with board and whether for reward or not, as may be required for the purposes of this Act or of the Children (Scotland) Act 1995;

(b) in the case of a residential establishment which is a grant-aided or independent school (as respectively defined in section 135(1) of the Education (Scotland) Act 1980), to that establishment if any part of its functions are as described in paragraph (a) above.";

1980 c. 44.

(b) in subsection (1A)—

(i) in paragraph (a) of the definition of "establishment", for the words "sections 61A and" there shall be substituted "section"; and

(ii) at the end of that definition there shall be added "but an establishment is not excluded for those purposes by paragraph (a) above by reason only of its being registrable by the Registrar of Independent Schools in Scotland;"; and

(c) in subsection (2), for the words "section 62(8) and (8A) below" there shall be substituted "sections 61A(1) and 62(8) and (8A) of this Act".

(3) For section 61A there shall be substituted—

"Voluntary registration.

61A.—(1) A grant-aided or independent school, provided it is not a residential establishment the whole or a substantial part of whose functions is as described in subsection (1)(a) of section 61 of this Act, may be carried on by a person without his being registered in respect of it as mentioned in subsection (2) of that section; but he may if he wishes apply in accordance with section 62, or as the case may be 63, of this Act for such registration.

(2) Sections 62(8) and (8A) and 65 of this Act shall not apply in relation to establishments as respects which registration has been by virtue of subsection (1) above.".

(4) After section 62 there shall be inserted—

"Certificate of registration as respects grant-aided or independent school.

62A. A certificate of registration granted under section 62 of this Act as respects an establishment which is a grant-aided, or independent, school shall relate to the whole of the establishment except so much as is used exclusively for educational purposes.".

(5) In section 65(1) (removal of persons from establishment), after the word "ought"—

(a) where it first occurs, there shall be inserted "(by virtue of subsections (2) and (3)) of section 61 of this Act)"; and

(b) where it occurs for the second time, there shall be inserted "(by virtue of the said subsections (2) and (3))".

(6) For section 67 there shall be substituted—

"Entry to examine state and management of establishments etc.

67.—(1) A person duly authorised by a local authority may in the area of that authority, at all reasonable times, enter, for a relevant purpose—

(a) any establishment as regards which a person is registered, or ought (by virtue of subsections (2) and (3) of section 61 of this Act) to be registered, under section 62 of this Act; or

(b) any place which the person so authorised has reasonable cause to believe is being used as such an establishment,

and subsections (2A) to (2D), (4) and (5) of section 6 of this Act shall apply in respect of a person so authorised as they apply in respect of a person duly authorised under subsection (1) of that section.

(2) "Relevant purpose" in subsection (1) above means—

(a) the purpose of making such examinations into the state and management of the establishment or place, and the condition and treatment of the persons in it, as the person so authorised thinks necessary; or

(b) the purpose of inspecting any records, or registers (in whatever form they are held) relating to the place, or to any person for whom, under or by virtue of this Act, section 7 (functions of local authorities) or 8 (provision of after-care services) of the Mental Health (Scotland) Act 1984, or Part II of the Children (Scotland) Act 1995, services are being or have been provided in the place.".

1984 c.36.
1995 c. 36.

35. After section 125 of the Education (Scotland) Act 1980 there shall be inserted—

Welfare of children in accommodation provided for purposes of school attendance.

1980 c. 44.

"Children and young persons in accommodation

Welfare of children and young persons in accommodation provided for purposes of school attendance.

125A. Where, for the purposes of his being in attendance at a school, a child or young person is provided with residential accommodation, in a place in or outwith that school, by—

(a) an education authority, the board of management of a self-governing school or the managers of a grant-aided or independent school; or

(b) by any other person in pursuance of arrangements made by any such authority, board of management or managers,

the authority, board of management or managers in question shall have the duty to safeguard and promote the welfare of the child or young person while he is so accommodated; and the powers of inspection exercisable by virtue of section 66(1) of this Act shall include the power to inspect the place to determine whether his welfare is adequately safeguarded and promoted there.".

Welfare of certain children in hospitals and nursing homes etc.

36.—(1) Where a child is provided with residential accommodation by a person mentioned in subsection (3) below and it appears to the person that the child either—

(a) has had no parental contact for a continuous period of three months or more; or

(b) is likely to have no parental contact for a period which, taken with any immediately preceding period in which the child has had no such contact, will constitute a continuous period of three months or more,

the person shall (whether or not the child has been, or will be, so accommodated throughout the continuous period) so notify the local authority in whose area the accommodation is provided.

(2) A local authority receiving notification under subsection (1) above shall—

(a) take such steps as are reasonably practicable to enable them to determine whether the child's welfare is adequately safeguarded and promoted while he is so accommodated; and

(b) consider the extent to which (if at all) they should exercise any of their functions under this Act with respect to the child.

(3) The persons are—

1978 c. 29.

(a) any health board constituted under section 2 of the National Health Service (Scotland) Act 1978;

(b) any national health service trust established under section 12A of that Act;

(c) any person carrying on—

1984 c. 36.

(i) a private hospital registered under Part IV of the Mental Health (Scotland) Act 1984; or

1938 c. 73.

(ii) a nursing home in respect of which either he is registered under section 1(3) of the Nursing Homes Registration (Scotland) Act 1938 or exemption has been granted under section 6 or 7 of that Act.

(4) For the purposes of subsection (1) above, a child has parental contact only when in the presence of a person having parental responsibilities in relation to him.

(5) A person duly authorised by a local authority may in the area of that authority, at all reasonable times, enter for the purposes of subsection (2) above or of determining whether there has been compliance with subsection (1) above any such place as is mentioned in sub-paragraph (i) or (ii) of subsection (3)(c) above and may for those purposes inspect any records or registers relating to that place; and

1968 c. 49.

subsections (2A) to (2D) and (4) of section 6 of the Social Work (Scotland) Act 1968 (exercise of powers of entry and inspection) shall apply in respect of a person so authorised as they apply in respect of a person duly authorised under subsection (1) of that section.

37. In paragraph 2 of Schedule 9 to the Children Act 1989 (which provides for regulations disqualifying certain persons from registration as a child minder or as a provider of day care for young children), at the end of sub-paragraph (1) there shall be added "unless he has—

(a) disclosed the fact to the appropriate local authority; and

(b) obtained their written consent.".

Modification of provisions of Children Act 1989 regarding disqualification from registration as child minder etc.

1989 c. 41.

Short-term refuges for children at risk of harm.

38.—(1) Where a child appears—

(a) to a local authority to be at risk of harm, they may at the child's request—

    (i) provide him with refuge in a residential establishment both controlled or managed by them and designated by them for the purposes of this paragraph; or

    (ii) arrange for a person whose household is approved by virtue of section 5(3)(b) of the Social Work (Scotland) Act 1968 (provision for securing that persons are not placed in any household unless the household has prescribed approval) and is designated by them for the purposes of this paragraph to provide him with refuge in that household,

for a period which does not exceed the relevant period;

1968 c. 49.

(b) to a person who carries on a residential establishment in respect of which the person is for the time being registered (as mentioned in section 61(2) of that Act), or to any person for the time being employed in the management of that establishment, to be at risk of harm, the person to whom the child so appears may at the child's request provide him with refuge, for a period which does not exceed the relevant period, in the establishment but shall do so only if and to the extent that the local authority within whose area the establishment is situated have given their approval to the use of the establishment (or a part of the establishment) for the purposes of this paragraph.

(2) The Secretary of State may by regulations make provision as to—

(a) designation, for the purposes of paragraph (a) of subsection (1) above, of establishments and households;

(b) application for, the giving of and the withdrawal of, approval under paragraph (b) of subsection (1) above;

(c) requirements (if any) which must be complied with while any such approval remains in force;

(d) the performance by a person mentioned in the said paragraph (b) of anything to be done by him under that paragraph;

(e) the performance by a local authority of their functions under this section; and

(f) the giving, to such persons or classes of person as may be specified in the regulations, of notice as to the whereabouts of a child provided with refuge under this section,

and regulations made under this subsection may include such incidental and supplementary provisions as he thinks fit.

(3) While a child is being provided with refuge under, and in accordance with regulations made under, this section, none of the enactments mentioned in subsection (4) below shall apply in relation to

him unless the commencement of the period of refuge has followed within two days of the termination of a prior period of refuge so provided to him by any person.

(4) The enactments are—

    (a) section 89 of this Act and, so far as it applies in relation to anything done in Scotland, section 83 of this Act; and

1969 c.54.

    (b) section 32(3) of the Children and Young Persons Act 1969 (compelling, persuading, inciting or assisting any person to be absent from detention etc.), so far as it applies in relation to anything done in Scotland.

(5) References in this section to the relevant period shall be construed as references either to a period which does not exceed seven days or, in such exceptional circumstances as the Secretary of State may prescribe, to a period which does not exceed fourteen days.

1984 c.56.

(6) A child who is provided with refuge for a period by virtue of such arrangements as are mentioned in subsection (1)(a) above shall not be regarded as a foster child for the purposes of the Foster Children (Scotland) Act 1984 by reason only of such provision.

CHAPTER 2

CHILDREN'S HEARINGS

Constitution of children's hearings

Formation of children's pa..l and children's hearings.

39.—(1) For every local government area there shall be a children's panel for the purposes of this Act, and any other enactment conferring powers on a children's hearing (or on such a panel).

(2) Schedule 1 to this Act shall have effect with respect to the recruitment, appointment, training and expenses of members of a children's panel and the establishment of Children's Panel Advisory Committees and joint advisory committees.

(3) Sittings of members of the children's panel (to be known as "children's hearings") shall be constituted from the panel in accordance with subsection (5) below.

(4) A children's hearing shall be constituted for the performance of the functions given to such a hearing by or by virtue of—

    (a) this Act; or

    (b) any other enactment conferring powers on a children's hearing.

(5) A children's hearing shall consist of three members, one of whom shall act as chairman; and shall not consist solely of male, or solely of female, members.

Qualifications, employment and duties of reporters

Qualification and employment of reporters.

40.—(1) The qualifications of a reporter shall be such as the Secretary of State may prescribe.

(2) A reporter shall not, without the consent of the Scottish Children's Reporter Administration, be employed by a local authority.

1975 c.21.

(3) The Secretary of State may make regulations in relation to the functions of any reporter under this Act and the Criminal Procedure (Scotland) Act 1975.

(4) The Secretary of State and the Lord Advocate may—

(a) by regulations empower a reporter, whether or not he is an advocate or solicitor, to conduct before a sheriff any proceedings which under this Chapter or Chapter 3 of this Part of this Act are heard by the sheriff;

(b) prescribe such requirements as they think fit as to qualifications, training or experience necessary for a reporter to be so empowered.

(5) In this section, "reporter" means—

(a) the Principal Reporter; or

(b) any officer of the Scottish Children's Reporter Administration to whom there is delegated, under section 131(1) of the Local Government etc. (Scotland) Act 1994, any of the functions which the Principal Reporter has under this or any other enactment.

1994 c.39.

Safeguards for children

41.—(1) Subject to subsection (2) below, in any proceedings under this Chapter or Chapter 3 of this Part of this Act either at a children's hearing or before the sheriff, the hearing or, as the case may be, the sheriff—

Safeguarding child's interests in proceedings.

(a) shall consider if it is necessary to appoint a person to safeguard the interests of the child in the proceedings; and

(b) if they, or he, so consider, shall make such an appointment, on such terms and conditions as appear appropriate.

(2) Subsection (1) above shall not apply in relation to proceedings under section 57 of this Act.

(3) Where a children's hearing make an appointment under subsection (1)(b) above, they shall state the reasons for their decision to make that appointment.

(4) The expenses of a person appointed under subsection (1) above shall—

(a) in so far as reasonably incurred by him in safeguarding the interests of the child in the proceedings, and

(b) except in so far as otherwise defrayed in terms of regulations made under section 101 of this Act,

be borne by the local authority—

(i) for whose area the children's panel from which the relevant children's hearing has been constituted is formed;

(ii) where there is no relevant children's hearing, within whose area the child resides.

(5) For the purposes of subsection (4) above, "relevant children's hearing" means, in the case of proceedings—

(a) at a children's hearing, that hearing;

(b) under section 68 of this Act, the children's hearing who have directed the application;

(c) on an appeal under section 51 of this Act, the children's hearing whose decision is being appealed against.

Conduct of proceedings at and in connection with children's hearing

Power of
Secretary of State
to make rules
governing
procedure at
children's hearing
etc.

42.—(1) Subject to the following provisions of this Act, the Secretary of State may make rules for constituting and arranging children's hearings and other meetings of members of the children's panel and for regulating their procedure.

(2) Without prejudice to the generality of subsection (1) above, rules under that subsection may make provision with respect to—

(a) the conduct of, and matters which shall or may be determined by, a business meeting arranged under section 64 of this Act;

(b) notification of the time and place of a children's hearing to the child and any relevant person in relation to the child and to such other persons as may be prescribed;

(c) how the grounds for referring the case to a children's hearing under section 65(1) of this Act are to be stated, and the right of the child and any such relevant person to dispute those grounds;

(d) the making available by the Principal Reporter, subject to such conditions as may be specified in the rules, of reports or information received by him to—

(i) members of the children's hearing;

(ii) the child concerned;

(iii) any relevant person; and

(iv) any other person or class of persons so specified;

(e) the procedure in relation to the disposal of matters arising under section 41(1) of this Act;

(f) the functions of any person appointed by a children's hearing under section 41(1) of this Act and any right of that person to information relating to the proceedings in question;

(g) the recording in writing of any statement given under section 41(3) of this Act;

(h) the right to appeal to the sheriff under section 51(1)(a) of this Act against a decision of the children's hearing and notification to such persons as may be prescribed of the proceedings before him;

(i) the right of the child and of any such relevant person to be represented at a children's hearing;

(j) the entitlement of the child, of any such relevant person and of any person who acts as the representative of the child or of any such relevant person to the refund of such expenses, incurred by the child or as the case may be the person or representative, as may be prescribed in connection with a children's hearing and with any proceedings arising from the hearing;

(k) persons whose presence shall be permitted at a children's hearing.

Privacy of
proceedings at and
right to attend
children's hearing.

43.—(1) Subject to subsection (3) below, a children's hearing shall be conducted in private, and, subject to any rules made under section 42 of this Act, no person other than a person whose presence is necessary for the proper consideration of the case which is being heard, or whose presence is permitted by the chairman, shall be present.

(2) The chairman shall take all reasonable steps to ensure that the number of persons present at a children's hearing at any one time is kept to a minimum.

(3) The following persons have the right to attend a children's hearing—

(a) a member of the Council on Tribunals, or of the Scottish Committee of that Council, in his capacity as such; and

(b) subject to subsection (4) below, a *bona fide* representative of a newspaper or news agency.

(4) A children's hearing may exclude a person described in subsection (3)(b) above from any part or parts of the hearing where, and for so long as, they are satisfied that—

(a) it is necessary to do so, in the interests of the child, in order to obtain the child's views in relation to the case before the hearing; or

(b) the presence of that person is causing, or is likely to cause, significant distress to the child.

(5) Where a children's hearing have exercised the power conferred by subsection (4) above to exclude a person, the chairman may, after that exclusion has ended, explain to the person the substance of what has taken place in his absence.

44.—(1) No person shall publish any matter in respect of proceedings at a children's hearing, or before a sheriff on an application under section 57, section 60(7), section 65(7) or (9), section 76(1) or section 85(1) of this Act, or on any appeal under this Part of this Act, which is intended to, or is likely to, identify—

Prohibition of publication of proceedings at children's hearing.

(a) any child concerned in the proceedings or appeal; or

(b) an address or school as being that of any such child.

(2) Any person who contravenes subsection (1) above shall be guilty of an offence and shall be liable on summary conviction to a fine not exceeding level 4 on the standard scale in respect of each such contravention.

(3) It shall be a defence in proceedings for an offence under this section for the accused to prove that he did not know, and had no reason to suspect, that the published matter was intended, or was likely, to identify the child or, as the case may be, the address or school.

(4) In this section "to publish" includes, without prejudice to the generality of that expression,—

(a) to publish matter in a programme service, as defined by section 201 of the Broadcasting Act 1990 (definition of programme service); and

1990 c.42.

(b) to cause matter to be published.

(5) The requirements of subsection (1) above may, in the interests of justice, be dispensed with by—

(a) the sheriff in any proceedings before him;

(b) the Court of Session in any appeal under section 51(11) of this Act; or

(c) the Secretary of State in relation to any proceedings at a children's hearing,

to such extent as the sheriff, the Court or the Secretary of State as the case may be considers appropriate.

45.—(1) Where a child has been notified in accordance with rules made under subsection (1) of section 42 of this Act by virtue of subsection (2)(b) of that section that his case has been referred to a children's hearing, he shall—

> (a) have the right to attend at all stages of the hearing; and
>
> (b) subject to subsection (2) below, be under an obligation to attend those stages in accordance with the notice.

(2) Without prejudice to subsection (1)(a) above and section 65(4) of this Act, where a children's hearing are satisfied—

> (a) in a case concerned with an offence mentioned in Schedule 1 to the Criminal Procedure (Scotland) Act 1975, that the attendance of the child is not necessary for the just hearing of that case; or
>
> (b) in any case, that it would be detrimental to the interests of the child for him to be present at the hearing of his case,

they may release the child from the obligation imposed by subsection (1)(b) above.

(3) Subject to subsection (2) above, the Principal Reporter shall be responsible for securing the attendance of the child at the hearing of his case by a children's hearing (and at any subsequent hearing to which the case is continued under section 69(1)(a) of this Act).

(4) On the application of the Principal Reporter, a children's hearing, if satisfied on cause shown that it is necessary for them to do so, may issue, for the purposes of subsection (3) above, a warrant under this subsection to find the child, to keep him in a place of safety and to bring him before a children's hearing.

(5) Where a child has failed to attend a children's hearing in accordance with such notice as is mentioned in subsection (1) above, they may, either on the application of the Principal Reporter or of their own motion, issue a warrant under this subsection, which shall have the same effect as a warrant under subsection (4) above.

(6) A child who has been taken to a place of safety under a warrant granted under this section shall not be kept there after whichever is the earlier of—

> (a) the expiry of seven days beginning on the day he was first so taken there; or
>
> (b) the day on which a children's hearing first sit to consider his case in accordance with subsection (7) below.

(7) Where a child has been found in pursuance of a warrant under this section and he cannot immediately be brought before a children's hearing, the Principal Reporter shall, wherever practicable, arrange a children's hearing to sit on the first working day after the child was so found.

Attendance of child and relevant person at children's hearing.

1975 c.21.

(8) Subject to section 46 of this Act, a person who is a relevant person as respects a child shall, where a children's hearing are considering the case of the child—

    (a) have the right to attend at all stages of the hearing; and

    (b) be obliged to attend at all stages of the hearing unless the hearing are satisfied that it would be unreasonable to require his attendance or that his attendance is unnecessary for the proper consideration of the case.

(9) Any person who fails to attend a hearing which, under subsection (8)(b) above, he is obliged to attend shall be guilty of an offence and shall be liable on summary conviction to a fine not exceeding level 3 on the standard scale.

46.—(1) Where a children's hearing are considering the case of a child in respect of whom a person is a relevant person, they may exclude that person, or that person and any representative of his, or any such representative, from any part or parts of the hearing for so long as is necessary in the interests of the child, where they are satisfied that— *Power to exclude relevant person from children's hearing.*

    (a) they must do so in order to obtain the views of the child in relation to the case before the hearing; or

    (b) the presence of the person or persons in question is causing, or is likely to cause, significant distress to the child.

(2) Where a children's hearing exercise the power conferred by subsection (1) above, the chairman of the hearing shall, after that exclusion has ended, explain to any person who was so excluded the substance of what has taken place in his absence.

47.—(1) Where a children's hearing has been arranged in respect of any person, the hearing— *Presumption and determination of age.*

    (a) shall, at the commencement of the proceedings, make inquiry as to his age and shall proceed with the hearing only if he declares that he is a child or they so determine; and

    (b) may, at any time before the conclusion of the proceedings, accept a declaration by the child, or make a fresh determination, as to his age.

(2) The age declared to, or determined by, a children's hearing to be the age of a person brought before them shall, for the purposes of this Part of this Act, be deemed to be the true age of that person.

(3) No decision reached, order continued, warrant granted or requirement imposed by a children's hearing shall be invalidated by any subsequent proof that the age of a person brought before them had not been correctly declared to the hearing or determined by them.

Transfer etc. of cases

48.—(1) Where a children's hearing are satisfied, in relation to a case which they are hearing, that it could be better considered by a children's hearing constituted from a children's panel for a different local government area, they may at any time during the course of the hearing request the Principal Reporter to arrange for such other children's hearing to dispose of the case. *Transfer of case to another children's hearing.*

(2) Where a case has been transferred in pursuance of subsection (1) above, the grounds of referral accepted or established for the case shall not require to be further accepted or established for the purposes of the children's hearing to which the case has been transferred.

Referral or remission to children's hearing where child guilty of an offence.

1975 c. 21.

49.—(1) In section 173 of the Criminal Procedure (Scotland) Act 1975 (reference or remission to children's hearing where child guilty of an offence: solemn proceedings), for subsections (1) to (3) there shall be substituted—

"(1) Where a person who is charged with an offence and pleads guilty to, or is found guilty of, that offence is a child who is not subject to a supervision requirement, the court on that plea or finding may—

(a) instead of making an order, remit the case to the Principal Reporter to arrange a children's hearing to dispose of the case; or

(b) request the Principal Reporter to arrange a children's hearing for the purpose of obtaining their advice as to the treatment of the child.

(2) Where a person, who is charged with an offence and pleads guilty to, or is found guilty of, that offence, is aged sixteen years or over and is subject to a supervision requirement, the court if it is—

(a) the High Court, may; and

(b) the sheriff court shall,

proceed in accordance with either paragraph (a) or (b) of subsection (1) above.

(3) Where a child who is charged with an offence and pleads guilty to, or is found guilty of, that offence—

(a) is aged under sixteen years; and

(b) is subject to a supervision requirement,

the court dealing with the case if it is—

(i) the High Court, may; and

(ii) the sheriff court, shall,

request the Principal Reporter to arrange a children's hearing for the purpose of obtaining their advice as to the treatment of the child.

(3A) Where a court has obtained the advice of a children's hearing in pursuance—

(a) of paragraph (b) of subsection (1) above; or

(b) of subsection (3) above,

the court, after consideration of the advice received from the children's hearing may, as it thinks proper, itself dispose of the case or remit the case as mentioned in paragraph (a) of the said subsection (1).".

(2) In section 372 of that Act (reference or remission to children's hearing where child guilty of an offence: summary proceedings), for subsections (1) to (3) there shall be substituted—

"(1) Where a person who is charged with an offence and pleads guilty to, or is found guilty of, that offence is a child who is not subject to a supervision requirement, the court on that plea or finding may—

(a) instead of making an order, remit the case to the Principal Reporter to arrange a children's hearing to dispose of the case; or

(b) request the Principal Reporter to arrange a children's hearing for the purpose of obtaining their advice as to the treatment of the child.

(2) Where a person, who is charged with an offence and pleads guilty to, or is found guilty of, that offence, is aged sixteen years or over and is subject to a supervision requirement, the court shall proceed in accordance with either paragraph (a) or (b) of subsection (1) above.

(3) Where a child who is charged with an offence and pleads guilty to, or is found guilty of, that offence—

(a) is aged under sixteen years; and

(b) is subject to a supervision requirement,

the court dealing with the case shall request the Principal Reporter to arrange a children's hearing for the purpose of obtaining their advice as to the treatment of the child.

(3A) Where a court has obtained the advice of a children's hearing in pursuance—

(a) of paragraph (b) of subsection (1) above; or

(b) of subsection (3) above,

the court, after consideration of the advice received from the children's hearing may, as it thinks proper, itself dispose of the case or remit the case as mentioned in paragraph (a) of the said subsection (1).".

50.—(1) Where a court has, under section 173, 372 or 373 of the Criminal Procedure (Scotland) Act 1975, remitted a case to a children's hearing for disposal, a certificate signed by the clerk of the court stating that the child or person concerned has pled guilty to, or has been found guilty of, the offence to which the remit relates shall be conclusive evidence for the purposes of the remit that the offence has been committed by the child or person.

Treatment of child's case on remission by court.
1975 c.21.

(2) Where a court has under the said section 373 remitted a case to a children's hearing for disposal, the provisions of this Act shall apply to the person concerned as if he were a child.

Appeals

51.—(1) Subject to subsection (15) below, a child or a relevant person (or relevant persons) or both (or all)—

(a) may, within a period of three weeks beginning with the date of any decision of a children's hearing, appeal to the sheriff against that decision; and

(b) where such an appeal is made, shall be heard by the sheriff.

Appeal against decision of children's hearing or sheriff.

(2) The Principal Reporter shall, in respect of any appeal under subsection (1) above, ensure that all reports and statements available to the hearing, along with the reports of their proceedings and the reasons for the decision, are lodged with the sheriff clerk.

(3) The sheriff may, on appeal under subsection (1) above, hear evidence from, or on behalf of, the parties in relation to the decision; and, without prejudice to that generality, the sheriff may—

    (a) examine the Principal Reporter;

    (b) examine the authors or compilers of any reports or statements; and

    (c) call for any further report which he considers may assist him in deciding the appeal.

(4) Where the sheriff decides that an appeal under this section has failed, he shall confirm the decision of the children's hearing.

(5) Where the sheriff is satisfied that the decision of the children's hearing is not justified in all the circumstances of the case he shall allow the appeal, and—

    (a) where the appeal is against a warrant to find and keep or, as the case may be, to keep a child in a place of safety, he shall recall the warrant;

    (b) where the child is subject to a supervision requirement containing a condition imposed under section 70(9) of this Act, he shall direct that the condition shall cease to have effect; and

    (c) in any case, he may, as he thinks fit—

        (i) remit the case with reasons for his decision to the children's hearing for reconsideration of their decision; or

        (ii) discharge the child from any further hearing or other proceedings in relation to the grounds for the referral of the case; or

        (iii) substitute for the disposal by the children's hearing any requirement which could be imposed by them under section 70 of this Act.

(6) Where a sheriff imposes a requirement under subsection (5)(c)(iii) above, that requirement shall for the purposes of this Act, except of this section, be treated as a disposal by the children's hearing.

(7) Where the sheriff is satisfied that an appeal under subsection (1) above against the decision of a children's hearing arranged under section 73(8) of this Act is frivolous, he may order that no subsequent appeal against a decision to continue (whether with or without any variation) the supervision requirement in question shall lie until the expiration of twelve months beginning with the date of the order.

(8) An appeal under subsection (1) above in respect of the issue of a warrant by a children's hearing shall be disposed of within three days of the lodging of the appeal; and failing such disposal the warrant shall cease to have effect at the end of that period.

(9) Where a child or a relevant person appeals under subsection (1) above against a decision of a children's hearing in relation to a supervision requirement, the child or the relevant person may make application to a children's hearing for the suspension of the requirement appealed against.

(10) It shall be the duty of the Principal Reporter forthwith to arrange a children's hearing to consider the application under subsection (9) above, and that hearing may grant or refuse the application.

(11) Subject to subsections (13) and (15) below, an appeal shall lie by way of stated case either on a point of law or in respect of any irregularity in the conduct of the case—

(a) to the sheriff principal from any decision of the sheriff—

(i) on an appeal under subsection (1) of this section;

(ii) on an application made under section 65(7) or (9) of this Act; or

(iii) on an application made under section 85(1) of this Act; and

(b) to the Court of Session from any decision of the sheriff such as is mentioned in sub-paragraphs (i) to (iii) of paragraph (a) above and, with leave of the sheriff principal, from any decision of the sheriff principal on an appeal under that paragraph; and the decision of the Court of Session in the matter shall be final.

(12) An appeal under subsection (11) above may be made at the instance of—

(a) the child or any relevant person, either alone or together; or

(b) the Principal Reporter on behalf of the children's hearing.

(13) An application to the sheriff, or as the case may be the sheriff principal, to state a case for the purposes of an appeal under subsection (11)(a) or (b) above shall be made within a period of twenty-eight days beginning with the date of the decision appealed against.

(14) On deciding an appeal under subsection (11) above the sheriff principal or as the case may be the Court of Session shall remit the case to the sheriff for disposal in accordance with such directions as the court may give.

(15) No appeal shall lie under this section in respect of—

(a) a decision of the sheriff on an application under section 57 of this Act; or

(b) a decision of a children's hearing continuing a child protection order under section 59(4) of this Act.

CHAPTER 3

PROTECTION AND SUPERVISION OF CHILDREN

Children requiring compulsory measures of supervision

52.—(1) The question of whether compulsory measures of supervision are necessary in respect of a child arises if at least one of the conditions mentioned in subsection (2) below is satisfied with respect to him.

Children requiring compulsory measures of supervision.

(2) The conditions referred to in subsection (1) above are that the child—

(a) is beyond the control of any relevant person;

(b) is falling into bad associations or is exposed to moral danger;

(c) is likely—

(i) to suffer unnecessarily; or

(ii) be impaired seriously in his health or development, due to a lack of parental care;

(d) is a child in respect of whom any of the offences mentioned in Schedule 1 to the Criminal Procedure (Scotland) Act 1975 (offences against children to which special provisions apply) has been committed;

1975 c.21.

(e) is, or is likely to become, a member of the same household as a child in respect of whom any of the offences referred to in paragraph (d) above has been committed;

(f) is, or is likely to become, a member of the same household as a person who has committed any of the offences referred in paragraph (d) above;

(g) is, or is likely to become, a member of the same household as a person in respect of whom an offence under sections 2A to 2C of the Sexual Offences (Scotland) Act 1976 (incest and intercourse with a child by step-parent or person in position of trust) has been committed by a member of that household;

1976 c.67.

(h) has failed to attend school regularly without reasonable excuse;

(i) has committed an offence;

(j) has misused alcohol or any drug, whether or not a controlled drug within the meaning of the Misuse of Drugs Act 1971;

1971 c.38.

(k) has misused a volatile substance by deliberately inhaling its vapour, other than for medicinal purposes;

(l) is being provided with accommodation by a local authority under section 25, or is the subject of a parental responsibilities order obtained under section 86, of this Act and, in either case, his behaviour is such that special measures are necessary for his adequate supervision in his interest or the interest of others.

(3) In this Part of this Act, "supervision" in relation to compulsory measures of supervision may include measures taken for the protection, guidance, treatment or control of the child.

Preliminary and investigatory measures

Provision of information to the Principal Reporter.

53.—(1) Where information is received by a local authority which suggests that compulsory measures of supervision may be necessary in respect of a child, they shall—

(a) cause inquiries to be made into the case unless they are satisfied that such inquiries are unnecessary; and

(b) if it appears to them after such inquiries, or after being satisfied that such inquiries are unnecessary, that such measures may be required in respect of the child, give to the Principal Reporter such information about the child as they have been able to discover.

(2) A person, other than a local authority, who has reasonable cause to believe that compulsory measures of supervision may be necessary in respect of a child—

(a) shall, if he is a constable, give to the Principal Reporter such information about the child as he has been able to discover;

(b) in any other case, may give the Principal Reporter that information.

(3) A constable shall make any report required to be made under paragraph (b) of section 17(1) of the Police (Scotland) Act 1967 (duty to make reports in relation to commission of offences) in relation to a child to the Principal Reporter as well as to the appropriate prosecutor.

1967 c.77.

(4) Where an application has been made to the sheriff—

    (a) by the Principal Reporter in accordance with a direction given by a children's hearing under section 65(7) or (9) of this Act; or

    (b) by any person entitled to make an application under section 85 of this Act,

the Principal Reporter may request any prosecutor to supply him with any evidence lawfully obtained in the course of, and held by the prosecutor in connection with, the investigation of a crime or suspected crime, being evidence which may assist the sheriff in determining the application; and, subject to subsection (5) below, it shall be the duty of the prosecutor to comply with such a request.]

(5) A prosecutor may refuse to comply with a request issued under subsection (4) above where he reasonably believes that it is necessary to retain the evidence for the purposes of any proceedings in respect of a crime, whether the proceedings have been commenced or are to be commenced by him.

(6) The Lord Advocate may direct that in any specified case or class of cases any evidence lawfully obtained in the course of an investigation of a crime or suspected crime shall be supplied, without the need for a request under subsection (4) above, to the Principal Reporter.

(7) In subsections (3), (4) and (5) above "crime" and "prosecutor" have the same meanings respectively given by section 462 of the Criminal Procedure (Scotland) Act 1975.

1975 c.21.

54.—(1) Where in any relevant proceedings it appears to the court that any of the conditions in section 52(2)(a) to (h), (j), (k) or (l) of this Act is satisfied with respect to a child, it may refer the matter to the Principal Reporter, specifying the condition.

Reference to the Principal Reporter by court.

(2) In this section "relevant proceedings" means—

    (a) an action for divorce or judicial separation or for declarator of marriage, nullity of marriage, parentage or non-parentage;

    (b) proceedings relating to parental responsibilities or parental rights within the meaning of Part I of this Act;

    (c) proceedings for an adoption order under the Adoption (Scotland) Act 1978 or for an order under section 18 of that Act declaring a child free for adoption; and

1978 c.28.

    (d) proceedings for an offence against section 35 (failure by parent to secure regular attendance by his child at a public school), 41 (failure to comply with attendance order) or 42(3) (failure to permit examination of child) of the Education (Scotland) Act 1980.

1980 c. 44.

(3) Where the court has referred a matter to the Principal Reporter under subsection (1) above, he shall—

    (a) make such investigation as he thinks appropriate; and

(b) if he considers that compulsory measures of supervision are necessary,

arrange a children's hearing to consider the case of the child under section 69 of this Act; and subsection (1) of that section shall apply as if the condition specified by the court under subsection (1) above were a ground of referral established in accordance with section 68 of this Act.

Child assessment orders.

55.—(1) A sheriff may grant an order under this section for an assessment of the state of a child's health or development, or of the way in which he has been treated (to be known as a "child assessment order"), on the application of a local authority if he is satisfied that—

(a) the local authority have reasonable cause to suspect that the child in respect of whom the order is sought is being so treated (or neglected) that he is suffering, or is likely to suffer, significant harm;

(b) such assessment of the child is required in order to establish whether or not there is reasonable cause to believe that the child is so treated (or neglected); and

(c) such assessment is unlikely to be carried out, or be carried out satisfactorily, unless the order is granted.

(2) Where—

(a) an application has been made under subsection (1) above; and

(b) the sheriff considers that the conditions for making a child protection order under section 57 of this Act are satisfied,

he shall make such an order under that section as if the application had been duly made by the local authority under that section rather than this section.

(3) A child assessment order shall—

(a) specify the date on which the assessment is to begin;

(b) have effect for such period as is specified in the order, not exceeding seven days beginning with the date specified by virtue of paragraph (a) above;

(c) require any person in a position to produce the child to—

(i) produce him to any authorised person;

(ii) permit that person or any other authorised person to carry out an assessment in accordance with the order; and

(iii) comply with any other conditions of the order; and

(d) be carried out by an authorised person in accordance with the terms of the order.

(4) A child assessment order may—

(a) where necessary, permit the taking of the child concerned to any place for the purposes of the assessment; and

(b) authorise the child to be kept at that place, or any other place, for such period of time as may be specified in the order.

(5) Where a child assessment order makes provision under subsection (4) above, it shall contain such directions as the sheriff considers appropriate as to the contact which the child shall be allowed to have with any other person while the child is in any place to which he has been taken or in which he is being kept under a child assessment order.

(6) In this section "authorised person" means any officer of the local authority, and any person authorised by the local authority to perform the assessment, or perform any part of it.

56.—(1) Where the Principal Reporter receives information from any source about a case which may require a children's hearing to be arranged he shall, after making such initial investigation as he thinks necessary, proceed with the case in accordance with subsection (4) or (6) below.

(2) For the purposes of making any initial investigation under subsection (1) above, the Principal Reporter may request from the local authority a report on the child and on such circumstances concerning the child as appear to him to be relevant; and the local authority shall supply the report which may contain such information, from any person whomsoever, as the Principal Reporter thinks, or the local authority think, fit.

(3) A report requested under subsection (2) above may contain information additional to that given by the local authority under section 53 of this Act.

(4) The Principal Reporter may decide, after an initial investigation under subsection (1) above, that a children's hearing does not require to be arranged; and where he so decides—

    (a) he shall inform the child, any relevant person and the person who brought the case to his notice, or any of those persons, that he has so decided; and

    (b) he may, if he considers it appropriate, refer the case to a local authority with a view to their making arrangements for the advice, guidance and assistance of the child and his family in accordance with Chapter 1 of this Part of this Act.

(5) Where the Principal Reporter has decided under subsection (4) above that a children's hearing does not require to be arranged, he shall not at any other time, on the basis solely of the information obtained during the initial investigation referred to in that subsection, arrange a children's hearing under subsection (6) below.

(6) Where it appears to the Principal Reporter that compulsory measures of supervision are necessary in respect of the child, he shall arrange a children's hearing to which he shall refer the case for consideration and determination.

(7) Where the Principal Reporter has arranged a children's hearing in accordance with subsection (6) above, he—

    (a) shall, where he has not previously done so, request a report under subsection (2) above;

    (b) may request from the local authority such information, supplementary or additional to a report requested under subsection (2) above, as he thinks fit;

and the local authority shall supply that report, or as the case may be information, and any other information which they consider to be relevant.

Child protection
orders.

Measures for the emergency protection of children

57.—(1) Where the sheriff, on an application by any person, is satisfied that—

    (a) there are reasonable grounds to believe that a child—

        (i) is being so treated (or neglected) that he is suffering significant harm; or

        (ii) will suffer such harm if he is not removed to and kept in a place of safety, or if he does not remain in the place where he is then being accommodated (whether or not he is resident there); and

    (b) an order under this section is necessary to protect that child from such harm (or such further harm),

he may make an order under this section (to be known as a "child protection order").

(2) Without prejudice to subsection (1) above, where the sheriff on an application by a local authority is satisfied—

    (a) that they have reasonable grounds to suspect that a child is being or will be so treated (or neglected) that he is suffering or will suffer significant harm;

    (b) that they are making or causing to be made enquiries to allow them to decide whether they should take any action to safeguard the welfare of the child; and

    (c) that those enquiries are being frustrated by access to the child being unreasonably denied, the authority having reasonable cause to believe that such access is required as a matter of urgency,

he may make a child protection order.

(3) Without prejudice to any additional requirement imposed by rules made by virtue of section 91 of this Act, an application for a child protection order shall—

    (a) identify—

        (i) the applicant; and

        (ii) in so far as practicable, the child in respect of whom the order is sought;

    (b) state the grounds on which the application is made; and

    (c) be accompanied by such supporting evidence, whether in documentary form or otherwise, as will enable the sheriff to determine the application.

(4) A child protection order may, subject to such terms and conditions as the sheriff considers appropriate, do any one or more of the following—

    (a) require any person in a position to do so to produce the child to the applicant;

    (b) authorise the removal of the child by the applicant to a place of safety, and the keeping of the child at that place;

    (c) authorise the prevention of the removal of the child from any place where he is being accommodated;

(d) provide that the location of any place of safety in which the child is being kept should not be disclosed to any person or class of person specified in the order.

(5) Notice of the making of a child protection order shall be given forthwith by the applicant to the local authority in whose area the child resides (where that authority is not the applicant) and to the Principal Reporter.

(6) In taking any action required or permitted by a child protection order or by a direction under section 58 of this Act the applicant shall only act where he reasonably believes that to do so is necessary to safeguard or promote the welfare of the child.

(7) Where by virtue of a child protection order a child is removed to a place of safety provided by a local authority, they shall, subject to the terms and conditions of that order and of any direction given under section 58 of this Act, have the like duties in respect of the child as they have under section 17 of this Act in respect of a child looked after by them.

58.—(1) When the sheriff makes a child protection order, he shall at that time consider whether it is necessary to give a direction to the applicant for the order as to contact with the child for— *Directions in relation to contact and exercise of parental responsibilities and parental rights.*

   (a) any parent of the child;

   (b) any person with parental responsibilities in relation to the child; and

   (c) any other specified person or class of persons;

and if he determines that there is such a necessity he may give such a direction.

(2) Without prejudice to the generality of subsection (1) above, a direction under that subsection may—

   (a) prohibit contact with the child for any person mentioned in paragraphs (a) to (c) of that subsection;

   (b) make contact with the child for any person subject to such conditions as the sheriff considers appropriate to safeguard and promote the welfare of the child.

(3) A direction under subsection (1) above may make different provision in relation to different persons or classes of person.

(4) A person applying for a child protection order under section 57(1) or (2) of this Act may at the same time apply to the sheriff for a direction in relation to the exercise or fulfilment of any parental responsibilities or parental rights in respect of the child concerned, if the person considers such a direction necessary to safeguard or promote the welfare of the child.

(5) Without prejudice to the generality of subsection (4) above, a direction under that subsection may be sought in relation to—

   (a) any examination as to the physical or mental state of the child;

   (b) any other assessment or interview of the child; or

   (c) any treatment of the child arising out of such an examination or assessment,

which is to be carried out by any person.

(6) The sheriff may give a direction sought under subsection (4) above where he considers there is a necessity such as is mentioned in that subsection; and such a direction may be granted subject to such conditions, if any, as the sheriff (having regard in particular to the duration of the child protection order to which it relates) considers appropriate.

(7) A direction under this section shall cease to have effect when—

(a) the sheriff, on an application under section 60(7) of this Act, directs that it is cancelled; or

(b) the child protection order to which it is related ceases to have effect.

Initial hearing of case of child subject to child protection order.

59.—(1) This section applies where—

(a) a child in respect of whom a child protection order has been made—

(i) has been taken to a place of safety by virtue of section 57(4)(b) of this Act; or

(ii) is prevented from being removed from any place by virtue of section 57(4)(c) of this Act;

(b) the Principal Reporter has not exercised his powers under section 60(3) of this Act to discharge the child from the place of safety; and

(c) the Principal Reporter has not received notice, in accordance with section 60(9) of this Act, of an application under subsection (7) of that section.

(2) Where this section applies, the Principal Reporter shall arrange a children's hearing to conduct an initial hearing of the child's case in order to determine whether they should, in the interests of the child, continue the child protection order under subsection (4) below.

(3) A children's hearing arranged under subsection (2) above shall take place on the second working day after that order is implemented.

(4) Where a children's hearing arranged under subsection (2) above are satisfied that the conditions for the making of a child protection order under section 57 of this Act are established, they may continue the child protection order and any direction given under section 58 of this Act (whether with or without variation of the order or, as the case may be, the direction) until the commencement of a children's hearing in relation to the child arranged in accordance with section 65(2) of this Act.

(5) In subsection (3) above, section 60 and section 65(2) of this Act any reference, in relation to the calculation of any period, to the time at which a child protection order is implemented shall be construed as a reference—

(a) in relation to such an order made under paragraph (b) of subsection (4) of section 57 of this Act, to the day on which the child was removed to a place of safety in accordance with the order; and

(b) in relation to such an order made under paragraph (c) of that subsection, to the day on which the order was made,

and "implement" shall be construed accordingly.

60.—(1) Where, by the end of twenty-four hours of a child protection order being made (other than by virtue of section 57(4)(c) of this Act), the applicant has made no attempt to implement the order it shall cease to have effect.

(2) Where an application made under subsection (7) below has not been determined timeously in accordance with subsection (8) below, the order to which the application relates shall cease to have effect.

(3) A child shall not be—

    (a) kept in a place of safety under a child protection order;

    (b) prevented from being removed from any place by such an order; or

    (c) subject to any term or condition contained in such an order or a direction given under section 58 of this Act,

where the Principal Reporter, having regard to the welfare of the child, considers that, whether as a result of a change in the circumstances of the case or of further information relating to the case having been received by the Principal Reporter, the conditions for the making of a child protection order in respect of the child are no longer satisfied or that the term, condition or direction is no longer appropriate and notifies the person who implemented the order that he so considers.

(4) The Principal Reporter shall not give notice under subsection (3) above where—

    (a) proceedings before a children's hearing arranged under section 59(2) of this Act in relation to the child who is subject to the child protection order have commenced; or

    (b) the hearing of an application made under subsection (7) of this section has begun.

(5) Where the Principal Reporter has given notice under subsection (3) above, he shall also, in such manner as may be prescribed, notify the sheriff who made the order.

(6) A child protection order shall cease to have effect—

    (a) where an initial hearing arranged under section 59(2) of this Act does not continue the order under subsection (4) of that section;

    (b) where an application is made to the sheriff under subsection (7) below, on the sheriff recalling such order under subsection (13) below;

    (c) on the person who implemented the order receiving notice from the Principal Reporter that he has decided not to refer the case of a child who is subject to the order to a children's hearing arranged in accordance with section 65(2) of this Act;

    (d) on the Principal Reporter giving notice in accordance with subsection (3) above in relation to the order that he considers that the conditions for the making of it are no longer satisfied; or

    (e) where such order is continued under section 59(4) of this Act or subsection (12)(d) below, on the commencement of a children's hearing arranged under section 65(2) of this Act.

(7) An application to the sheriff to set aside or vary a child protection order made under section 57 of this Act or a direction given under section

58 of this Act or such an order or direction continued (whether with or without variation) under section 59(4) of this Act, may be made by or on behalf of—

    (a) the child to whom the order or direction relates;

    (b) a person having parental rights over the child;

    (c) a relevant person;

    (d) any person to whom notice of the application for the order was given by virtue of rules; or

    (e) the applicant for the order made under section 57 of this Act.

(8) An application under subsection (7) above shall be made—

    (a) in relation to a child protection order made under section 57, or a direction given under section 58, of this Act, before the commencement of a children's hearing arranged in accordance with section 59(2) of this Act; and

    (b) in relation to such an order or direction continued (whether with or without variation) by virtue of subsection (4) of the said section 59, within two working days of such continuation,

and any such application shall be determined within three working days of being made.

(9) Where an application has been made under subsection (7) above, the applicant shall forthwith give notice, in a manner and form prescribed by rules, to the Principal Reporter.

(10) At any time which is—

    (a) after the giving of the notice required by subsection (9) above; but

    (b) before the sheriff has determined the application in accordance with subsection (11) below,

the Principal Reporter may arrange a children's hearing the purpose of which shall be to provide any advice they consider appropriate to assist the sheriff in his determination of the application.

(11) The sheriff shall, after hearing the parties to the application and, if he wishes to make representations, the Principal Reporter, determine whether—

    (a) the conditions for the making of a child protection order under section 57 of this Act are satisfied; or

    (b) where the application relates only to a direction under section 58 of this Act, the direction should be varied or cancelled.

(12) Where the sheriff determines that the conditions referred to in subsection (11)(a) above are satisfied, he may—

    (a) confirm or vary the order, or any term or condition on which it was granted;

    (b) confirm or vary any direction given, in relation to the order, under section 58 of this Act;

    (c) give a new direction under that section; or

    (d) continue in force the order and any such direction until the commencement of a children's hearing arranged in accordance with section 65(2) of this Act.

(13) Where the sheriff determines that the conditions referred to in subsection (11)(a) above are not satisfied he shall recall the order and cancel any direction given under section 58 of this Act.

61.—(1) Where, on the application of any person, a justice of the peace is satisfied—

    (a) both that the conditions laid down for the making of a child protection order in section 57(1) of this Act are satisfied and that it is probable that any such order, if made, would contain an authorisation in terms of paragraph (b) or (c) of subsection (4) of that section; but

    (b) that it is not practicable in the circumstances for an application for such an order to be made to the sheriff or for the sheriff to consider such an application,

he may grant to the applicant an authorisation under this section.

Emergency protection of children where child protection order not available.

(2) Where on the application of a local authority a justice of the peace is satisfied—

    (a) both that the conditions laid down for the making of a child protection order in section 57(2) of this Act are satisfied and that it is probable that any such order, if made, would contain an authorisation in terms of paragraph (b) or (c) of subsection (4) of that section; but

    (b) that it is not practicable in the circumstances for an application for such an order to be made to the sheriff or for the sheriff to consider such an application,

he may grant an authorisation under this section.

(3) An authorisation under this section may—

    (a) require any person in a position to do so to produce the child to the applicant;

    (b) prevent any person from removing a child from a place where he is then being accommodated;

    (c) authorise the applicant to remove the child to a place of safety and to keep him there until the expiration of the authorisation.

(4) An authorisation under this section shall cease to have effect—

    (a) twelve hours after being made, if within that time—

        (i) arrangements have not been made to prevent the child's removal from any place specified in the authorisation; or

        (ii) he has not been, or is not being, taken to a place of safety; or

    (b) where such arrangements have been made or he has been so taken when—

        (i) twenty-four hours have expired since it was so given; or

        (ii) an application for a child protection order in respect of the child is disposed of,

    whichever is the earlier.

(5) Where a constable has reasonable cause to believe that—

    (a) the conditions for the making of a child protection order laid down in section 57(1) are satisfied;

(b) that it is not practicable in the circumstances for him to make an application for such an order to the sheriff or for the sheriff to consider such an application; and

(c) that, in order to protect the child from significant harm (or further such harm), it is necessary for him to remove the child to a place of safety,

he may remove the child to such a place and keep him there.

(6) The power conferred by subsection (5) above shall not authorise the keeping of a child in a place of safety for more than twenty-four hours from the time when the child is so removed.

(7) The authority to keep a child in a place of safety conferred by subsection (5) above shall cease on the disposal of an application in relation to the child for a child protection order.

(8) A child shall not be—

(a) kept in a place of safety; or

(b) prevented from being removed from any place,

under this section where the Principal Reporter considers that the conditions for the grant of an authorisation under subsection (1) or (2) above or the exercise of the power conferred by subsection (5) above are not satisfied, or that it is no longer in the best interests of the child that he should be so kept.

Regulations in respect of emergency child protection measures.

62.—(1) The Secretary of State may make regulations concerning the duties in respect of a child of any person removing him to, and keeping him in, a place of safety under section 61 above.

(2) Regulations under this section may make provision requiring—

(a) notification of the removal of a child to be given to a person specified in the regulations;

(b) intimation to be given to any person of the place of safety at which a child is being kept;

(c) notification to be given to any person of the ceasing to have effect, under section 61(4)(a) of this Act, of an authorisation.

Children arrested by the police

Review of case of child arrested by police.

1975 c. 21.

63.—(1) Where the Principal Reporter has been informed by a constable, in accordance with section 296(3) of the Criminal Procedure (Scotland) Act 1975, that charges are not to be proceeded with against a child who has been detained in a place of safety in accordance with that section, the Principal Reporter shall, unless he considers that compulsory measures of supervision are not required in relation to the child, arrange a children's hearing to which he shall refer the case.

(2) A children's hearing arranged under subsection (1) above shall begin not later than the third day after the Principal Reporter received the information mentioned in that subsection.

(3) Where the Principal Reporter considers that a child of whose detention he has been informed does not require compulsory measures of supervision, he shall direct that the child shall no longer be kept in the place of safety.

(4) Subject to subsection (3) above, a child who has been detained in a place of safety may continue to be kept at that place until the commencement of a children's hearing arranged under subsection (1) above.

(5) Subject to subsection (6) below, a children's hearing arranged under subsection (1) above may—

> (a) if they are satisfied that the conditions mentioned in subsection (2) of section 66 of this Act are satisfied, grant a warrant to keep the child in a place of safety; and

> (b) direct the Principal Reporter to arrange a children's hearing for the purposes of section 65(1) of this Act,

and subsections (3) to (8) of the said section 66 shall apply to a warrant granted under this subsection as they apply to a warrant granted under subsection (1) of the said section 66.

(6) A child shall not be kept in a place of safety in accordance with a warrant granted under subsection (5) above where the Principal Reporter, having regard to the welfare of the child, considers that, whether as a result of a change in the circumstances of the case or of further information relating to the case having been received by the Principal Reporter—

> (a) the conditions mentioned in section 66(2) of this Act are no longer satisfied in relation to the child; or

> (b) the child is not in need of compulsory measures of supervision,

and where he does so consider he shall give notice to that effect to the person who is keeping the child in that place in accordance with the warrant.

Business meeting preparatory to children's hearing

64.—(1) At any time prior to the commencement of proceedings at the children's hearing, the Principal Reporter may arrange a meeting with members of the children's panel from which the children's hearing is to be constituted under section 39(4) of this Act for those proceedings (any such meeting being, in this Part of this Act referred to as a "business meeting"). *Business meeting preparatory to children's hearing.*

(2) Where a business meeting is arranged under subsection (1) above, the Principal Reporter shall give notice to the child in respect of whom the proceedings are to be commenced and any relevant person in relation to the child—

> (a) of the arrangement of the meeting and of the matters which may be considered and determined by the meeting;

> (b) of their right to make their views on those matters known to the Principal Reporter; and

> (c) of the duty of the Principal Reporter to present those views to the meeting.

(3) A business meeting, subject to subsection (4) below—

> (a) shall determine such procedural and other matters as may be prescribed by rules under subsection (1) of section 42 of this Act by virtue of subsection (2)(a) of that section; and

(b) may give such direction or guidance to the Principal Reporter in relation to the performance of his functions in relation to the proceedings as they think appropriate.

(4) Before a business meeting makes such a determination or gives such direction or guidance to the Principal Reporter, the Principal Reporter shall present, and they shall consider, any views expressed to him by virtue of subsection (2)(b) above.

(5) Subject to any rules made under section 42(1) of this Act by virtue of subsection (2)(a) of that section and with the exception of sections 44 and, as regards any determination made by the business meeting under subsection (3)(a) above, 51, the provisions of this Act which relate to a children's hearing shall not apply to a business meeting.

Referral to, and disposal of case by, children's hearing

Referral to, and proceedings at, children's hearing.

65.—(1) The Principal Reporter shall refer to the children's hearing, for consideration and determination on the merits, the case of any child in respect of whom he is satisfied that—

(a) compulsory measures of supervision are necessary, and

(b) at least one of the grounds specified in section 52(2) of this Act is established;

and he shall state such grounds in accordance with rules made under section 42(1) of this Act by virtue of subsection (2)(c) of that section.

(2) Where a referral is made in respect of a child who is subject to a child protection order made under section 57, and that order is continued under section 59(4) or 60(12)(d), of this Act, the Principal Reporter shall arrange for the children's hearing under subsection (1) above to take place on the eighth working day after the order was implemented.

(3) Where a referral is made in respect of a child who is subject to a supervision requirement, the children's hearing shall, before disposing of the referral in accordance with section 69(1)(b) or (c) of this Act, review that requirement in accordance with subsections (9) to (12) of section 73 of this Act.

(4) Subject to subsections (9) and (10) below, it shall be the duty of the chairman of the children's hearing to whom a child's case has been referred under subsection (1) above to explain to the child and the relevant person, at the opening of proceedings on the referral, the grounds stated by the Principal Reporter for the referral in order to ascertain whether these grounds are accepted in whole or in part by them.

(5) Where the chairman has given the explanation required by subsection (4) above and the child and the relevant person accept the grounds for the referral, the children's hearing shall proceed in accordance with section 69 of this Act.

(6) Where the chairman has given the explanation required by subsection (4) above and the child and the relevant person accept the grounds in part, the children's hearing may, if they consider it appropriate to do so, proceed in accordance with section 69 of this Act with respect to those grounds which are accepted.

(7) Where the chairman has given the explanation required under subsection (4) above and either or both of the child and the relevant person—

   (a) do not accept the grounds for the referral; or

   (b) accept the grounds in part, but the children's hearing do not consider it appropriate to proceed with the case under subsection (6) above,

the hearing shall either direct the Principal Reporter to make an application to the sheriff for a finding as to whether such grounds for the referral as are not accepted by the child and the relevant person are established or shall discharge the referral.

(8) Subject to subsection (10) below, it shall be the duty of the chairman to explain to the child and to the relevant person the purpose for which the application to the sheriff is being made and to inform the child that he is under an obligation to attend the hearing before the sheriff.

(9) Where a children's hearing are satisfied that the child—

   (a) for any reason will not be capable of understanding the explanation of the grounds for the referral required under subsection (4) above; or

   (b) has not understood an explanation given under that subsection,

they shall either direct the Principal Reporter to make an application to the sheriff for a finding as to whether any of the grounds of the referral are established or discharge the referral.

(10) The acceptance by the relevant person of the grounds of the referral shall not be a requirement for a children's hearing proceeding under this section to consider a case where that person is not present.

66.—(1) Without prejudice to any other power enjoyed by them under this Part of this Act and subject to subsection (5) below, a children's hearing—

   (a) arranged to consider a child's case under this Part of this Act; and

   (b) unable to dispose of the case,

may, if they are satisfied that one of the conditions mentioned in subsection (2) below is met, grant a warrant under this subsection.

Warrant to keep child where children's hearing unable to dispose of case.

(2) The conditions referred to in subsection (1) above are—

   (a) that there is reason to believe that the child may—

      (i) not attend at any hearing of his case; or

      (ii) fail to comply with a requirement under section 69(3) of this Act; or

   (b) that it is necessary that the child should be kept in a place of safety in order to safeguard or promote his welfare.

(3) A warrant under subsection (1) above may require any person named in the warrant—

   (a) to find and to keep or, as the case may be, to keep the child in a place of safety for a period not exceeding twenty-two days after the warrant is granted;

   (b) to bring the child before a children's hearing at such times as may be specified in the warrant.

(4) A warrant under subsection (1) above may contain such conditions as appear to the children's hearing to be necessary or expedient, and without prejudice to that generality may—

    (a) subject to section 90 of this Act, require the child to submit to any medical or other examination or treatment; and

    (b) regulate the contact with the child of any specified person or class of persons.

(5) Subject to subsection (8) below, at any time prior to its expiry, a warrant granted under this section may, on an application to the children's hearing, on cause shown by the Principal Reporter, be continued in force, whether with or without variation of any condition imposed by virtue of subsection (4) above, by the children's hearing for such further period, not exceeding twenty-two days, as appears to them to be necessary.

(6) Where a children's hearing are satisfied that either of the criteria specified in section 70(10) of this Act are satisfied, they may order that, pending the disposal of his case, the child shall be liable to be placed and kept in secure accommodation within a residential establishment at such times as the person in charge of that establishment, with the agreement of the chief social work officer of the relevant local authority, considers necessary.

(7) Where a children's hearing grant a warrant under subsection (1) above or continue such a warrant under subsection (5) above, they may order that the place of safety at which the child is to be kept shall not be disclosed to any person or class of persons specified in the order.

(8) A child shall not be kept in a place of safety or secure accommodation by virtue of this section for a period exceeding sixty-six days from the day when he was first taken to a place of safety under a warrant granted under subsection (1) above.

Warrant for further detention of child.

67.—(1) Where a child is being kept in a place of safety by virtue of a warrant granted under section 66 of this Act or under this subsection, the Principal Reporter at any time prior to the expiry of that warrant may apply to the sheriff for a warrant to keep the child in that place after the warrant granted under the said section 66 or, as the case may be, this subsection has expired.

(2) A warrant under subsection (1) above shall only be granted on cause shown and—

    (a) shall specify the date on which it will expire; and

    (b) may contain any such requirement or condition as may be contained in a warrant granted under the said section 66.

(3) Where the sheriff grants a warrant under subsection (1) above, he may also make an order under this subsection in such terms as are mentioned in subsection (6) or (7) of the said section 66; and any order under this subsection shall cease to have effect when the warrant expires.

(4) An application under subsection (1) above may be made at the same time as, or during the hearing of, an application which the Principal Reporter has been directed by a children's hearing to make under section 65(7) or (9) of this Act.

68.—(1) This section applies to applications under subsections (7) and (9) of section 65 of this Act and a reference in this section (except in subsection (8)) to "an application" is a reference to an application under either of those subsections.

(2) An application shall be heard by the sheriff within twenty-eight days of its being lodged.

(3) Where one of the grounds for the referral to which an application relates is the condition referred to in section 52(2)(i)—

(a) the application shall be made to the sheriff who would have jurisdiction if the child were being prosecuted for that offence; and

(b) in hearing the application in relation to that ground, the standard of proof required in criminal proceedings shall apply.

(4) A child shall—

(a) have the right to attend the hearing of an application; and

(b) subject to subsection (5) below, be under an obligation to attend such hearing;

and without prejudice to the right of each of them to be legally represented, the child and the relevant person may be represented by a person other than a legally qualified person at any diet fixed by the sheriff for the hearing of the application.

(5) Without prejudice to subsection (4)(a) above, the sheriff may dispense with the obligation imposed by subsection (4)(b) above where he is satisfied—

(a) in an application in which the ground of referral to be established is a condition mentioned in section 52(2)(d), (e), (f) or (g) of this Act, that the obligation to attend of the child is not necessary for the just hearing of that application; and

(b) in any application, that it would be detrimental to the interests of the child for him to be present at the hearing of the application.

(6) Where the child fails to attend the hearing of an application at which his attendance has not been dispensed with under subsection (5) above, the sheriff may grant an order to find and keep the child; and any order under this subsection shall be authority for bringing the child before the sheriff and, subject to subsection (7) below, for keeping him in a place of safety until the sheriff can hear the application.

(7) The child shall not be kept in a place of safety by virtue of subsection (6) above after whichever is the earlier of—

(a) the expiry of fourteen days beginning with the day on which the child is found; or

(b) the disposal of the application by the sheriff.

(8) Where in the course of the hearing of an application—

(a) under section 65(7) of this Act, the child and the relevant person accept any of the grounds for referral to which the application relates, the sheriff shall; or

(b) under section 65(9) of this Act, the relevant person accepts any of the grounds for referral to which the application relates, the sheriff may, if it appears to him reasonable to do so,

dispense with the hearing of evidence relating to that ground and deem the ground to be established for the purposes of the application, unless he is satisfied that, in all the circumstances of the case, the evidence should be heard.

(9) Where a sheriff decides that none of the grounds for referral in respect of which an application has been made are established, he shall dismiss the application, discharge the referral to the children's hearing in respect of those grounds and recall, discharge or cancel any order, warrant, or direction under this Chapter of this Act which relates to the child in respect of those grounds.

(10) Where the sheriff, after the hearing of any evidence or on acceptance in accordance with subsection (8) above, finds that any of the grounds for the referral to which the application relates is, or should be deemed to be, established—

(a) he shall remit the case to the Principal Reporter to make arrangements for a children's hearing to consider and determine the case; and

(b) he may if he is satisfied that—

(i) keeping the child in a place of safety is necessary in the child's best interests; or

(ii) there is reason to believe that the child will run away before the children's hearing sit to consider the case,

issue an order requiring, subject to subsection (12) below, that the child be kept in a place of safety until the children's hearing so sit.

(11) An order issued under subsection (10) above may, if the sheriff is satisfied that either of the criteria mentioned in section 70(10) of this Act is fulfilled, provide that the child shall be liable to be placed and kept in secure accommodation within a residential establishment at such times as the person in charge of the establishment, with the agreement of the chief social work officer of the relevant local authority, considers necessary.

(12) A child shall not be kept in a place of safety by virtue of subsection (10)(b) above after whichever is the earlier of the following—

(a) the expiry of three days beginning with the day on which he is first so kept; or

(b) the consideration of his case by the children's hearing arranged under subsection (10)(a) above.

Continuation or disposal of referral by children's hearing.

69.—(1) Where the grounds of referral of the child's case stated by the Principal Reporter are accepted or are established in accordance with section 68 or section 85 of this Act, the children's hearing shall consider those grounds, any report obtained under section 56(7) of this Act and any other relevant information available to them and shall—

(a) continue the case to a subsequent hearing in accordance with subsection (2) below;

(b) discharge the referral of the case in accordance with subsection (12) below; or

(c) make a supervision requirement under section 70 of this Act.

(2) The children's hearing may continue the case to a subsequent hearing under this subsection where they are satisfied that, in order to complete their consideration of the case, it is necessary to have a further investigation of the case.

(3) Where a children's hearing continue the case under subsection (2) above, they may, for the purposes of the investigation mentioned by that subsection, require the child to attend, or reside at, any clinic, hospital or other establishment during a period not exceeding twenty-two days.

(4) Where a child fails to fulfil a requirement made under subsection (3) above, the children's hearing may, either on an application by the Principal Reporter or of their own motion, grant a warrant under this subsection.

(5) A warrant under subsection (4) above shall be authority—

(a) to find the child;

(b) to remove the child to a place of safety and keep him there; and

(c) where the place of safety is not the clinic, hospital or other establishment referred to in the requirement made under subsection (3) above, to take the child from the place of safety to such clinic, hospital or other establishment for the purposes of the investigation mentioned in subsection (2) above.

(6) A warrant under subsection (4) above shall be granted for such period as appears to the children's hearing to be appropriate, provided that no warrant shall permit the keeping of a child in a place of safety after whichever is the earlier of—

(a) the expiry of twenty-two days after the warrant is granted; or

(b) the day on which the subsequent hearing of the child's case by a children's hearing begins.

(7) Where a child's case has been continued under subsection (2) above and the children's hearing are satisfied that—

(a) keeping the child in a place of safety is necessary in the interests of safeguarding or promoting the welfare of the child; or

(b) there is reason to believe that the child may not attend the subsequent hearing of his case,

they may grant a warrant requiring that the child be taken to and kept in a place of safety.

(8) A warrant under subsection (7) above shall cease to have effect on whichever is the earlier of—

(a) the expiry of twenty-two days after the warrant is granted; or

(b) the day on which the subsequent hearing of the child's case by a children's hearing begins.

(9) A warrant under subsection (4) or (7) above may contain such conditions as appear to the children's hearing to be necessary or expedient, and without prejudice to that generality may—

(a) subject to section 90 of this Act, require the child to submit to any medical or other examination or treatment;

(b) regulate the contact with the child of any specified person or class of persons.

(0) Where a child is to be kept at a place of safety under a warrant nted under this section or is to attend, or reside at, any place in cordance with a requirement made under subsection (3) above, the hildren's hearing may order that such place shall not be disclosed to any person or class of persons specified in the order.

(11) Where a child is to reside in a residential establishment by virtue of a requirement made or warrant granted under this section, the children's hearing may, if satisfied that either of the criteria mentioned in section 70(10) of this Act is fulfilled, order that while the requirement or warrant remains in effect he shall be liable to be placed in secure accommodation within that establishment at such times as the person in charge of the establishment, with the agreement of the chief social work officer of the relevant local authority, considers necessary.

(12) Where a children's hearing decide not to make a supervision requirement under section 70 of this Act they shall discharge the referral.

(13) On the discharge of the referral of the child's case any order, direction, or warrant under Chapter 2, or this Chapter, of this Act in respect of the child's case shall cease to have effect.

Disposal of referral by children's hearing: supervision requirements, including residence in secure accommodation.

70.—(1) Where the children's hearing to whom a child's case has been referred under section 65(1) of this Act are satisfied that compulsory measures of supervision are necessary in respect of the child they may make a requirement under this section (to be known as a "supervision requirement").

(2) A children's hearing, where they decide to make such a requirement, shall consider whether to impose any condition such as is described in subsection (5)(b) below.

(3) A supervision requirement may require the child—

(a) to reside at any place or places specified in the requirement; and

(b) to comply with any condition contained in the requirement.

(4) The place or, as the case may be, places specified in a requirement under subsection (3)(a) above may, without prejudice to the generality of that subsection, be a place or places in England or Wales; and a supervision requirement shall be authority for the person in charge of such a place to restrict the child's liberty to such extent as that person may consider appropriate, having regard to the terms of the requirement.

(5) A condition imposed under subsection (3)(b) above may, without prejudice to the generality of that subsection—

(a) subject to section 90 of this Act, require the child to submit to any medical or other examination or treatment;

(b) regulate the contact with the child of any specified person or class of persons.

(6) A children's hearing may require, when making a supervision requirement, that any place where the child is to reside in accordance with the supervision requirement shall not be disclosed to any person specified in the requirement under this subsection or class of persons so specified.

(7) A children's hearing who make a supervision requirement may determine that the requirement shall be reviewed at such time during the duration of the requirement as they determine.

(8) A supervision requirement shall be in such form as the Secretary of State may prescribe by rules.

(9) Where a children's hearing are satisfied—

(a) that it is necessary to make a supervision requirement which includes a requirement under subsection (3)(a) above that the child reside in a named residential establishment; and

(b) that any of the criteria specified in subsection (10) below are satisfied,

they may specify in the requirement that the child shall be liable to be placed and kept in secure accommodation in that establishment during such period as the person in charge of that establishment, with the agreement of the chief social work officer of the relevant local authority, considers necessary.

(10) The criteria referred to in subsection (9) above are that the child—

(a) having previously absconded, is likely to abscond unless kept in secure accommodation, and, if he absconds, it is likely that his physical, mental or moral welfare will be at risk; or

(b) is likely to injure himself or some other person unless he is kept in such accommodation. ⏋

71.—(1) The relevant local authority shall, as respects a child subject to a supervision requirement, give effect to the requirement.

(2) Where a supervision requirement provides that the child shall reside—

(a) in relevant accommodation; or

(b) in any other accommodation not provided by a local authority,

the relevant local authority shall from time to time investigate whether, while the child is so resident, any conditions imposed by the supervision requirement are being fulfilled; and may take such steps as they consider reasonable if they find that such conditions are not being fulfilled.

(3) In this section, "relevant accommodation" means accommodation provided by the parents or relatives of the child or by any person associated with them or with the child.

Duties of local authority with respect to supervision requirements.

72.—(1) In any case of urgent necessity, where it is in the interests of—

(a) a child who is required by a supervision requirement imposed under section 70(3)(a) of this Act to reside in a specific residential establishment or specific other accommodation; or

(b) other children in that establishment or accommodation,

the chief social work officer of the relevant local authority may direct that, notwithstanding that requirement, the child be transferred to another place.

(2) Any child transferred under subsection (1) above shall have his case reviewed, in accordance with section 73(8) of this Act, by a children's hearing within seven days of his transfer.

Transfer of child subject to supervision requirement in case of necessity.

73.—(1) No child shall continue to be subject to a supervision requirement for any period longer than is necessary in the interests of promoting or safeguarding his welfare.

Duration and review of supervision requirement.

PART II

(2) Subject to any variation or continuation of a supervision requirement under subsection (9) below, no supervision requirement shall remain in force for a period longer than one year.

(3) A supervision requirement shall cease to have effect in respect of a child not later than on his attaining the age of eighteen years.

(4) A relevant local authority shall refer the case of a child who is subject to a supervision requirement to the Principal Reporter where they are satisfied that—

    (a) the requirement in respect of the child ought to cease to have effect or be varied;

    (b) a condition contained in the requirement is not being complied with; or

    (c) the best interests of the child would be served by their—

        (i) applying under section 86 of this Act for a parental responsibilities order;

1978 c.28.   (ii) applying under section 18 of the Adoption (Scotland) Act 1978 for an order freeing the child for adoption; or

        (iii) placing the child for adoption,

    and they intend to apply for such an order or so place the child.

(5) Where the relevant local authority are aware that an application has been made and is pending, or is about to be made, under section 12 of the said Act of 1978 for an adoption order in respect of a child who is subject to a supervision requirement, they shall forthwith refer his case to the Principal Reporter.

(6) A child or any relevant person may require a review of a supervision requirement in respect of the child at any time at least three months after—

    (a) the date on which the requirement is made; or

    (b) the date of the most recent continuation, or variation, by virtue of this section of the requirement.

(7) Where a child is subject to a supervision requirement and, otherwise than in accordance with that requirement or with an order under section 11 of this Act, a relevant person proposes to take the child to live outwith Scotland, the person shall, not later than twenty-eight days before so taking the child, give notice of that proposal in writing to the Principal Reporter and to the relevant local authority.

(8) The Principal Reporter shall—

    (a) arrange for a children's hearing to review any supervision requirement in respect of a child where—

        (i) the case has been referred to him under subsection (4) or (5) above;

        (ii) the review has been required under subsection (6) above;

        (iii) the review is required by virtue of section 70(7) or section 72(2) of this Act;

        (iv) he has received in respect of the child such notice as is mentioned in subsection (7) above; or

        (v) in any other case, the supervision requirement will expire within three months; and

(b) make any arrangements incidental to that review.

(9) Where a supervision requirement is reviewed by a children's hearing arranged under subsection (8) above, they may—

(a) where they are satisfied that in order to complete the review of the supervision requirement it is necessary to have a further investigation of the child's case, continue the review to a subsequent hearing;

(b) terminate the requirement;

(c) vary the requirement;

(d) insert in the requirement any requirement which could have been imposed by them under section 70(3) of this Act; or

(e) continue the requirement, with or without such variation or insertion.

(10) Subsections (3) to (10) of section 69 of this Act shall apply to a continuation under paragraph (a) of subsection (9) above of a review of a supervision requirement as they apply to the continuation of a case under subsection (1)(a) of that section.

(11) Where a children's hearing vary or impose a requirement under subsection (9) above which requires the child to reside in any specified place or places, they may order that such place or places shall not be disclosed to any person or class of persons specified in the requirement.

(12) Where a children's hearing is arranged under subsection (8)(a)(v) above, they shall consider whether, if the supervision requirement is not continued, the child still requires supervision or guidance; and where a children's hearing consider such supervision or guidance is necessary, it shall be the duty of the local authority to provide such supervision or guidance as the child is willing to accept.

(13) Where a children's hearing is arranged by virtue of subsection (4)(c) or (5) above, then irrespective of what the hearing do under subsection (9) above they shall draw up a report which shall provide advice in respect of, as the case may be, the proposed application under section 86 of this Act or under section 18 of the said Act of 1978, or the proposed placing for adoption or the application, or prospective application, under section 12 of that Act, for any court which may subsequently require to come to a decision, in relation to the child concerned, such as is mentioned in subsection (14) below.

(14) A court which is considering whether, in relation to a child, to grant an application under section 86 of this Act or under section 18 or 12 of the said Act of 1978 and which, by virtue of subsection (13) above, receives a report as respects that child, shall consider the report before coming to a decision in the matter.

74. The Secretary of State may by regulations provide—

(a) for the transmission of information regarding a child who is subject to a supervision requirement to any person who, by virtue of that requirement, has, or is to have, control over the child;

(b) for the temporary accommodation, where necessary, of a child so subject; and

(c) for the conveyance of a child so subject—

Further provision as respects children subject to supervision requirements.

(i) to any place in which, under the supervision requirement, he is to reside;

(ii) to any place to which he falls to be taken under subsection (1) or (5) of section 82 of this Act; or

(iii) to any person to whom he falls to be returned under subsection (3) of that section.

Powers of Secretary of State with respect to secure accommodation.

75—(1) The Secretary of State may by regulations make provision with respect to the placing in secure accommodation of any child—

(a) who is subject to a requirement imposed under section 70(3)(a) of this Act but not subject to a requirement under subsection (9) of that section; or

(b) who is not subject to a supervision requirement but who is being looked after by a local authority in pursuance of such enactments as may be specified in the regulations.

(2) Regulations under subsection (1) above may—

(a) specify the circumstances in which a child may be so placed under the regulations;

(b) make provision to enable a child who has been so placed or any relevant person to require that the child's case be brought before a children's hearing within a shorter period than would apply under regulations made under subsection (3) below; and

(c) specify different circumstances for different cases or classes of case.

(3) Subject to subsection (4) below and without prejudice to subsection (2)(b) above, the Secretary of State may prescribe—

(a) the maximum period during which a child may be kept under this Act in secure accommodation without the authority of a children's hearing or of the sheriff;

(b) the period within which a children's hearing shall be arranged to consider the case of a child placed in secure accommodation by virtue of regulations made under this section (and different periods may be so prescribed in respect of different cases or classes of case).

(4) Subsection (8) of section 66 of this Act shall apply in respect of a child placed in secure accommodation under regulations made under this section as if such placing took place by virtue of that section.

(5) The Secretary of State may by regulations vary the period within which a review of a condition imposed under section 70(9) of this Act shall be reviewed under section 73 of this Act.

(6) The Secretary of State may by regulations make provision for the procedures to be applied in placing children in secure accommodation; and without prejudice to the generality of this subsection, such regulations may—

(a) specify the duties of the Principal Reporter in relation to the placing of children in secure accommodation;

(b) make provision for the referral of cases to a children's hearing for review; and

(c) make provision for any person with parental responsibilities in relation to the child to be informed of the placing of the child in secure accommodation.

Exclusion orders

76.—(1) Subject to subsections (3) to (9) below, where on the application of a local authority the sheriff is satisfied, in relation to a child, that the conditions mentioned in subsection (2) below are met, he may grant an order under this section (to be known as "an exclusion order") excluding from the child's family home any person named in the order (in this Part of this Act referred to as the "named person").

(2) The conditions are—

(a) that the child has suffered, is suffering, or is likely to suffer, significant harm as a result of any conduct, or any threatened or reasonably apprehended conduct, of the named person;

(b) that the making of an exclusion order against the named person—

(i) is necessary for the protection of the child, irrespective of whether the child is for the time being residing in the family home; and

(ii) would better safeguard the child's welfare than the removal of the child from the family home; and

(c) that, if an order is made, there will be a person specified in the application who is capable of taking responsibility for the provision of appropriate care for the child and any other member of the family who requires such care and who is, or will be, residing in the family home (in this section, sections 77 to 79 and section 91(3)(f) of this Act referred to as an "appropriate person").

(3) No application under subsection (1) above for an exclusion order shall be finally determined under this section unless—

(a) the named person has been afforded an opportunity of being heard by, or represented before, the sheriff; and

(b) the sheriff has considered any views expressed by any person on whom notice of the application has been served in accordance with rules making such provision as is mentioned in section 91(3)(d) of this Act.

(4) Where, on an application under subsection (1) above, the sheriff—

(a) is satisfied as mentioned in that subsection; but

(b) the conditions mentioned in paragraphs (a) and (b) of subsection (3) above for the final determination of the application are not fulfilled,

he may grant an interim order, which shall have effect as an exclusion order pending a hearing by the sheriff under subsection (5) below held within such period as may be specified in rules made by virtue of section 91(3)(e) of this Act.

(5) The sheriff shall conduct a hearing under this subsection within such period as may be specified in rules made by virtue of section 91(3)(e) of this Act, and, if satisfied at that hearing as mentioned in subsection (1)

above, he may, before finally determining the application, confirm or vary the interim order, or any term or condition on which it was granted, or may recall such order.

(6) Where the conditions mentioned in paragraphs (a) and (b) of subsection (3) above have been fulfilled, the sheriff may, at any point prior to the final determination of the application, grant an interim order.

(7) An order under subsection (5) or (6) above shall have effect as an exclusion order pending the final determination of the application.

(8) Where—

(a) an application is made under subsection (1) above; and

(b) the sheriff considers that the conditions for making a child protection order under section 57 of this Act are satisfied,

he may make an order under that section as if the application had been duly made by the local authority under that rather than under this section.

(9) The sheriff shall not make an exclusion order if it appears to him that to do so would be unjustifiable or unreasonable, having regard to—

(a) all the circumstances of the case, including without prejudice to the generality of this subsection the matters specified in subsection (10) below; and

(b) any requirement such as is specified in subsection (11) below and the likely consequences in the light of that requirement of the exclusion of the named person from the family home.

(10) The matters referred to in subsection (9)(a) above are—

(a) the conduct of the members of the child's family (whether in relation to each other or otherwise);

(b) the respective needs and financial resources of the members of that family;

(c) the extent (if any) to which—

(i) the family home; and

(ii) any relevant item in that home,

is used in connection with a trade, business or profession by any member of the family.

(11) The requirement referred to in subsection (9)(b) above is a requirement that the named person (whether alone or with any other person) must reside in the family home, where that home—

(a) is or is part of an agricultural holding within the meaning of the Agricultural Holdings (Scotland) Act 1991; or

1991 c.55.

(b) is let, or is a home in respect of which possession is given, to the named person (whether alone or with any other person) by an employer as an incident of employment.

(12) In this Part of this Act—

"caravan" has the meaning given to it by section 29(1) of the Caravan Sites and Control of Development Act 1960;

1960 c.62.

"exclusion order", includes an interim order granted under subsection (4) above and such an order confirmed or varied under subsection (5) above and an interim order granted under subsection (6) above; except that in subsection (3) above and in section 79 of this Act, it does not include an interim order granted under subsection (4) above;

"family" has the meaning given in section 93(1) of this Act;

"family home" means any house, caravan, houseboat or other structure which is used as a family residence and in which the child ordinarily resides with any person described in subsection (13) below and the expression includes any garden or other ground or building attached to and usually occupied with, or otherwise required for the amenity or convenience of, the house, caravan, houseboat or other structure.

(13) The description of person referred to in the definition of "family home" in subsection (12) above, is a person who has parental responsibilities in relation to the child, or who ordinarily (and other than by reason only of his employment) has charge of, or control over him.

77.—(1) An exclusion order shall, in respect of the home to which it relates, have the effect of suspending the named person's rights of occupancy (if any) and shall prevent him from entering the home, except with the express permission of the local authority which applied for the order.

Effect of, and orders etc. ancillary to, exclusion order.

(2) The sheriff, on the application of the local authority, may, if and in so far as he thinks fit, when making an exclusion order do any of the things mentioned in subsection (3) below.

(3) The things referred to in subsection (2) above are—

(a) grant a warrant for the summary ejection of the named person from the home;

(b) grant an interdict prohibiting the named person from entering the home without the express permission of the local authority;

(c) grant an interdict prohibiting the removal by the named person of any relevant item specified in the interdict from the home, except either—

(i) with the written consent of the local authority, or of an appropriate person; or

(ii) by virtue of a subsequent order of the sheriff;

(d) grant an interdict prohibiting the named person from entering or remaining in a specified area in the vicinity of the home;

(e) grant an interdict prohibiting the taking by the named person of any step of a kind specified in the interdict in relation to the child;

(f) make an order regulating the contact between the child and the named person,

and the sheriff may make any other order which he considers is necessary for the proper enforcement of a remedy granted by virtue of paragraph (a), (b) or (c) of this subsection.

(4) No warrant, interdict or order (except an interdict granted by virtue of paragraph (b) of subsection (3) above) shall be granted or made under subsection (2) above if the named person satisfies the sheriff that it is unnecessary to do so.

(5) Where the sheriff grants a warrant of summary ejection under subsection (2) above in the absence of the named person, he may give directions as to the preservation of any of that person's goods and effects which remain in the family home.

(6) The sheriff may make an order of the kind specified in subsection (3)(f) above irrespective of whether there has been an application for such an order.

(7) On the application of either the named person or the local authority, the sheriff may make the exclusion order, or any remedy granted under subsection (2) above, subject to such terms and conditions as he considers appropriate.

(8) In this Part of this Act references to a "relevant item" are references to any item within the home which both—

    (a) is owned or hired by any member of the family concerned or an appropriate person or is being acquired by any such member or person under a hire purchase agreement or conditional sale agreement; and

    (b) is reasonably necessary to enable the home to be used as a family residence,

but does not include any such vehicle, caravan or houseboat or such other structure so used as is mentioned in the definition of "family home" in section 76(12) of this Act.

Powers of arrest etc. in relation to exclusion order.

78.—(1) The sheriff may, whether or not on an application such as is mentioned in subsection (2) below, attach a power of arrest to any interdict granted under section 77(2) of this Act by virtue of subsection (3) of that section.

(2) A local authority may at any time while an exclusion order has effect apply for such attachment of a power of arrest as is mentioned in subsection (1) above.

(3) A power of arrest attached to an interdict by virtue of subsection (1) above shall not have effect until such interdict, together with the attached power of arrest, is served on the named person.

(4) If, by virtue of subsection (1) above, a power of arrest is attached to an interdict, the local authority shall, as soon as possible after the interdict, together with the attached power of arrest, is served on the named person, ensure that there is delivered—

    (a) to the chief constable of the police area in which the family home is situated; and

    (b) where the interdict was granted by virtue of section 77(3)(e) of this Act, to the chief constable of the area in which the step or conduct which is prevented by the interdict may take place,

a copy of the application for the interdict and of the interlocutor granting the interdict together with a certificate of service of the interdict and, where the application to attach the power of arrest was made after the interdict was granted, a copy of that application and of the interlocutor above granting it and a certificate of service of the interdict together with the attached power of arrest.

(5) Where any interdict to which a power of arrest is attached by virtue of subsection (1) above is varied or recalled, the person who applied for

the variation or recall shall ensure that there is delivered to each chief constable specified in subsection (4) above a copy of the application for such variation or recall and of the interlocutor granting the variation or recall.

(6) A constable may arrest without warrant the named person if he has reasonable cause for suspecting that person to be in breach of an interdict to which a power of arrest has been attached by virtue of subsection (1) above.

(7) Where a person has been arrested under subsection (6) above, the constable in charge of a police station may—

> (a) if satisfied there is no likelihood of that person further breaching the interdict to which the power of arrest was attached under subsection (1) above, liberate him unconditionally; or

> (b) refuse to liberate that person.

(8) Such a refusal to liberate an arrested person as is mentioned in subsection (7)(b) above, and the detention of that person until his appearance in court by virtue of either subsection (11) below, or any provision of the Criminal Procedure (Scotland) Act 1975, shall not subject that constable to any claim whatsoever. 1975 c. 21.

(9) Where a person has been liberated under subsection (7)(a) above, the facts and circumstances which gave rise to the arrest shall be reported to the procurator fiscal forthwith.

(10) Subsections (11) to (13) below apply only where—

> (a) the arrested person has not been released under subsection (7)(a) above; and

> (b) the procurator fiscal decides that no criminal proceedings are to be taken in respect of the facts and circumstances which gave rise to the arrest.

(11) A person arrested under subsection (6) above shall, wherever practicable, be brought before the sheriff sitting as a court of summary criminal jurisdiction for the district in which he was arrested not later than in the course of the first day after the arrest, such day not being a Saturday, a Sunday or a court holiday prescribed for that court under section 10 of the Bail etc. (Scotland) Act 1980, on which the sheriff is not 1980 c.4. sitting for the disposal of criminal business.

(12) Subsections (1) and (3) of section 3 of the Criminal Justice 1980 c.62. (Scotland) Act 1980 (intimation to a person named by the person arrested) shall apply to a person arrested under subsection (6) above as they apply to a person who has been arrested in respect of an offence.

(13) Where a person is brought before the sheriff under subsection (11) above—

> (a) the procurator fiscal shall present to the court a petition containing—

>> (i) a statement of the particulars of the person arrested under subsection (6) above;

>> (ii) a statement of the facts and circumstances which gave rise to that arrest; and

>> (iii) a request that the person be detained for a further period not exceeding two days;

    (b) the sheriff, if it appears to him that—

        (i) the statement referred to in paragraph (a)(ii) above discloses a *prima facie* breach of interdict by the arrested person;

        (ii) proceedings for breach of interdict will be taken; and

        (iii) there is a substantial risk of violence by the arrested person against any member of the family, or an appropriate person, resident in the family home,

    may order the arrested person to be detained for a period not exceeding two days; and

    (c) the sheriff shall, in any case in which paragraph (b) above does not apply, order the release of the arrested person from custody (unless that person is in custody in respect of some other matter);

and in computing the period of two days referred to in paragraphs (a) and (b) above, no account shall be taken of a Saturday, a Sunday or any holiday in the court in which proceedings for breach of interdict will require to be raised.

    (14) Where a person—

    (a) is liberated under subsection (7)(a) above; or

    (b) is to be brought before the sheriff under subsection (11) above,

the procurator fiscal shall at the earliest opportunity, and, in the case of a person to whom paragraph (b) above applies, before that person is brought before the sheriff, take all reasonable steps to intimate to—

    (i) the local authority which made the application for the interdict;

    (ii) an appropriate person who will reside in, or who remains in residence in, the family home mentioned in the order; and

    (iii) any solicitor who acted for the appropriate person when the interdict was granted or to any other solicitor who the procurator fiscal has reason to believe acts for the time being for that person,

that he has decided that no criminal proceedings should be taken in respect of the facts and circumstances which gave rise to the arrest of the named person.

Duration, variation and recall of exclusion order.

    79.—(1) Subject to subsection (2) below, an exclusion order shall cease to have effect on a date six months after being made.

    (2) An exclusion order shall cease to have effect on a date prior to the date mentioned in subsection (1) above where—

    (a) the order contains a direction by the sheriff that it shall cease to have effect on that prior date;

    (b) the sheriff, on an application under subsection (3) below, recalls the order before the date so mentioned; or

    (c) any permission given by a third party to the spouse or partner of the named person, or to an appropriate person, to occupy the home to which the order relates is withdrawn.

    (3) The sheriff may, on the application of the local authority, the named person, an appropriate person or the spouse or partner of the named person, if that spouse or partner is not excluded from the family

home and is not an appropriate person, vary or recall an exclusion order and any warrant, interdict, order or direction granted or made under section 77 of this Act.

(4) For the purposes of this section, partners are persons who live together in a family home as if they were husband and wife.

80.—(1) The Secretary of State may make regulations with respect to the powers, duties and functions of local authorities in relation to exclusion orders.

Exclusion orders: supplementary provisions.

(2) An application for an exclusion order, or under section 79(3) of this Act for the variation or recall of such an order or of any thing done under section 77(2) of this Act, shall be made to the sheriff for the sheriffdom within which the family home is situated.

Offences in connection with orders etc. for protection of children

81. A person who intentionally obstructs—

(a) any person acting under a child protection order;

(b) any person acting under an authorisation granted under section 61(1) or (2) of this Act; or

(c) a constable acting under section 61(5) of this Act,

shall, subject to section 38(3) and (4) of this Act, be guilty of an offence and shall be liable on summary conviction to a fine not exceeding level 3 on the standard scale.

Offences in connection with orders etc. for protection of children.

Fugitive children and harbouring

82.—(1) A child who absconds—

(a) from a place of safety in which he is being kept under or by virtue of this Part of this Act;

(b) from a place (in this section referred to as a "relevant place") which, though not a place of safety such as is mentioned in paragraph (a) above, is a residential establishment in which he is required to reside by virtue of section 70(3)(a) of this Act or a hospital or other institution in which he is temporarily residing while subject to such a requirement; or

(c) from a person who, by virtue of a supervision requirement or of section 74 of this Act, has control over him while he is being taken to, is awaiting being taken to, or (whether or not by reason of being on leave) is temporarily away from, such place of safety or relevant place,

Recovery of certain fugitive children.

may be arrested without warrant in any part of the United Kingdom and taken to the place of safety or as the case may be the relevant place; and a court which is satisfied that there are reasonable grounds for believing that the child is within any premises may, where there is such power of arrest, grant a warrant authorising a constable to enter those premises and search for the child using reasonable force if necessary.

(2) Without prejudice to the generality of subsection (1) above, a child who at the end of a period of leave from a place of safety or relevant place fails to return there shall, for the purposes of this section, be taken to have absconded.

(3) A child who absconds from a person who, not being a person mentioned in paragraph (c) of subsection (1) above, is a person who has control over him by virtue of a supervision requirement may, subject to the same provisions as those to which an arrest under that subsection is subject, be arrested as is mentioned in that subsection and returned to that person; and the provision in that subsection for a warrant to be granted shall apply as respects such a child as it applies as respects a child mentioned in that subsection.

(4) If a child—

(a) is taken under subsection (1) above to a place of safety or relevant place; or

(b) is returned under subsection (3) above to a person,

but the occupier of that place of safety or of that relevant place, or as the case may be that person, is unwilling or unable to receive him, that circumstance shall be intimated forthwith to the Principal Reporter.

(5) Where intimation is required by subsection (4) above as respects a child, he shall be kept in a place of safety until—

(a) in a case where he is subject to a supervision requirement, he can be brought before a children's hearing for that requirement to be reviewed; or

(b) in any other case, the Principal Reporter has, in accordance with section 56(6) of this Act, considered whether compulsory measures of supervision are required in respect of him.

Harbouring.

83. A person who—

(a) knowingly assists or induces a child to abscond in circumstances which render the child liable to arrest under subsection (1) or (3) of section 82 of this Act;

(b) knowingly and persistently attempts to induce a child so to abscond;

(c) knowingly harbours or conceals a child who has so absconded; or

(d) knowingly prevents a child from returning—

(i) to a place mentioned in paragraph (a) or (b) of the said subsection (1);

(ii) to a person mentioned in paragraph (c) of that subsection, or in the said subsection (3),

1989 c.41.
S.I. 1995/755
(N.I.2)

shall, subject to section 38(3) and (4) of this Act, to section 51(5) and (6) of the Children Act 1989 and to Article 70(5) and (6) of the Children (Northern Ireland) Order 1995 (analogous provision for England and Wales and for Northern Ireland), be guilty of an offence and liable on summary conviction to a fine not exceeding level 5 on the standard scale or to imprisonment for a term not exceeding six months or to both such fine and such imprisonment.

Implementation of authorisations etc.

Implementation of authorisations etc.

84. Where an order, authorisation or warrant under this Chapter or Chapter 2 of this Part of this Act grants power to find a child and to keep him in a place of safety, such order, authorisation or warrant may be implemented as if it were a warrant for the apprehension of an accused person issued by a court of summary jurisdiction; and any enactment or rule of law applying to such a warrant shall, subject to the provisions of this Act, apply in like manner to the order, authorisation or warrant.

New evidence: review of establishment of grounds of referral

85.—(1) Subject to subsections (3) and (4) below, where subsection (2) below applies an application may be made to the sheriff for a review of a finding such as is mentioned in section 68(10) of this Act.

Application for review of establishment of grounds of referral.

(2) This subsection applies where the sheriff, on an application made by virtue of subsection (7) or (9) of section 65 of this Act (in this section referred to as the "original application"), finds that any of the grounds of referral is established.

(3) An application under subsection (1) above may only be made where the applicant claims—

(a) to have evidence which was not considered by the sheriff on the original application, being evidence the existence or significance of which might materially have affected the determination of the original application;

(b) that such evidence—

(i) is likely to be credible and reliable; and

(ii) would have been admissible in relation to the ground of referral which was found to be established on the original application; and

(c) that there is a reasonable explanation for the failure to lead such evidence on the original application.

(4) An application under subsection (1) above may only be made by—

(a) the child in respect of whom the ground of referral was found to be established; or

(b) any person who is a relevant person in relation to that child.

(5) Where the sheriff on an application under subsection (1) above is not satisfied that any of the claims made in the application are established he shall dismiss the application.

(6) Where the sheriff is satisfied on an application under subsection (1) above that the claims made in the application are established, he shall consider the evidence and if, having considered it, he is satisfied that—

(a) none of the grounds of referral in the original application to which the application relates is established, he shall allow the application, discharge the referral to the children's hearing in respect of those grounds and proceed in accordance with subsection (7) below in relation to any supervision requirement made in respect of the child (whether or not varied under section 73 of this Act) in so far as it relates to any such ground; or

(b) any ground of referral in the original application to which the application relates is established, he may proceed in accordance with section 68(10) of this Act.

(7) Where the sheriff is satisfied as is mentioned in subsection (6)(a) above, he may—

(a) order that any supervision requirement so mentioned shall terminate—

(i) immediately; or

(ii) on such date as he may specify; or

(b) if he is satisfied that there is evidence sufficient to establish any ground of referral, being a ground which was not stated in the original application, find such ground established and proceed in accordance with section 68(10) of this Act in relation to that ground.

(8) Where the sheriff specifies a date for the termination of a supervision requirement in accordance with subsection (7)(a)(ii) above, he may, before such termination, order a variation of that requirement, of any requirement imposed under subsection (6) of section 70 of this Act, or of any determination made under subsection (7) of that section; and such variation may take effect—

(a) immediately; or

(b) on such date as he may specify.

(9) Where the sheriff orders the termination of a supervision requirement in accordance with subsection (7)(a) above, he shall consider whether, after such termination, the child concerned will still require supervision or guidance; and where he considers that such supervision or guidance will be necessary he shall direct a local authority to provide it in accordance with subsection (10) below.

(10) Where a sheriff has given a direction under subsection (9) above, it shall be the duty of the local authority to comply with that direction; but that duty shall be regarded as discharged where they offer such supervision or guidance to the child and he, being a child of sufficient age and maturity to understand what is being offered, is unwilling to accept it.

CHAPTER 4

PARENTAL RESPONSIBILITIES ORDERS, ETC.

Parental responsibilities orders

Parental
responsibilities
order: general.

86.—(1) On the application of a local authority the sheriff may make an order transferring (but only during such period as the order remains in force) the appropriate parental rights and responsibilities relating to a child to them; and any such order shall be known as a "parental responsibilities order".

(2) A parental responsibilities order shall not be made unless the sheriff is satisfied that each relevant person either—

(a) freely, and with full understanding of what is involved, agrees unconditionally that the order be made; or

(b) is a person who—

(i) is not known, cannot be found or is incapable of giving agreement;

(ii) is withholding such agreement unreasonably;

(iii) has persistently failed, without reasonable cause, to fulfil one or other of the following parental responsibilities in relation to the child, that is to say the responsibility to safeguard and promote the child's health, development and welfare or, if the child is not living with him, the responsibility to maintain personal relations and direct contact with the child on a regular basis; or

(iv) has seriously ill-treated the child, whose reintegration into the same household as that person is, because of the serious ill-treatment or for other reasons, unlikely.

(3) The reference in subsection (1) above to the appropriate parental rights and responsibilities relating to the child is to all parental rights and responsibilities except any right to agree, or decline to agree—

(a) to the making of an application in relation to the child under section 18 (freeing for adoption) or 55 (adoption abroad) of the Adoption Act 1976, under section 18 or 49 of the Adoption (Scotland) Act 1978 or under Article 17, 18 or 57 of the Adoption (Northern Ireland) Order 1987 (corresponding provision for Scotland and Northern Ireland); or

1976 c. 36.
1978 c. 28.
S.I. 1987/2203
(N.I. 22)

(b) to the making of an adoption order.

(4) A person is a relevant person for the purposes of this section if he is a parent of the child or a person who for the time being has parental rights in relation to the child.

(5) The sheriff may, in an order under this section, impose such conditions as he considers appropriate; and he may vary or discharge such an order on the application of the local authority, of the child, of any person who immediately before the making of the order is a relevant person or of any other person claiming an interest.

(6) An order under this section shall, if not first discharged by the sheriff, terminate on the occurrence of any of the following—

(a) the child attains the age of eighteen years;

(b) he becomes the subject—

(i) of an adoption order within the meaning of the Adoption (Scotland) Act 1978; or

(ii) of an order under section 18 (freeing for adoption) or 55 (adoption abroad) of the Adoption Act 1976, under section 18 or 49 of the said Act of 1978 or under Article 17, 18 or 57 of the Adoption (Northern Ireland) Order 1987 (corresponding provision for Scotland and Northern Ireland);

(c) an order is made for his return under Part I of the Child Abduction and Custody Act 1985; or

1985 c.60.

(d) a decision, other than a decision mentioned in section 25(2) of the said Act of 1985 (decisions relating to rights of access), is registered with respect to him under section 16 of that Act.

87.—(1) Subject to subsections (2) and (3) below, where a parental responsibilities order is made as respects a child it shall be the duty of the local authority which applied for it (in this section and in section 88 of this Act referred to as the "appropriate authority") to fulfil the transferred responsibilities while the order remains in force.

Further provision as respects parental responsibilities orders.

(2) Notwithstanding that a parental responsibilities order has been made as respects a child, the appropriate authority may allow, either for a fixed period or until the authority otherwise determine, the child to reside with a parent, guardian, relative or friend of his in any case where it appears to the authority that so to allow would be for the benefit of the child.

(3) Without prejudice to any other provision of this Part of this Act, where by virtue of subsection (2) above a child is residing with a person, the appropriate authority may by notice in writing to the person require him to return the child to them by a time specified in the notice; and service of such notice shall be effected either by the authority leaving it in the person's hands or by their sending it to him, at his and the child's most recent known address, by recorded delivery service.

(4) For the purposes of any application for a parental responsibilities order, rules shall provide for the appointment, in such cases as are prescribed by such rules—

(a) of a person to act as curator *ad litem* to the child in question at the hearing of the application, safeguarding the interests of the child in such manner as may be so prescribed; and

(b) of a person (to be known as a "reporting officer") to witness agreements to parental responsibilities orders and to perform such other duties as may be so prescribed,

but one person may, as respects the child, be appointed both under paragraph (a) and under paragraph (b) above; so however that, where the applicant is a local authority, no employee of theirs shall be appointed under either or both of those paragraphs.

(5) Rules may provide for a person to be appointed reporting officer before the application in question is made.

Parental contact.

88.—(1) This section applies where a parental responsibilities order is being made, or as the case may be is in force, as respects a child.

(2) The child shall, subject to subsection (3) below, be allowed reasonable contact by the appropriate authority with—

(a) each person who, immediately before the making of the parental responsibilities order, is a relevant person for the purposes of section 86 of this Act as respects the child; and

(b) where, immediately before that order was made—

(i) a residence order or contact order was in force with respect to the child, the person in whose favour the residence order or contact order was made;

(ii) a person was entitled to have the child residing with him under an order by a court of competent jurisdiction, that person.

(3) Without prejudice to subsection (4) below, on an application made to him by the child, by the appropriate authority or by any person with an interest, the sheriff may make such order as he considers appropriate as to the contact, if any, which is to be allowed between the child and any person specified in the order (whether or not a person described in paragraphs (a) and (b) of subsection (2) above).

(4) A sheriff, on making a parental responsibilities order, or at any time while such an order remains in force as respects a child, may make an order under subsection (3) above as respects the child even where no application has been made to him in that regard.

(5) An order under this section may impose such conditions as the sheriff considers appropriate; and he may vary or discharge such an order on the application of the child, the appropriate authority or any person with an interest.

(6) An order under this section shall, if not first discharged by the sheriff, terminate when the parental responsibilities order to which it is referable does.

89. Any person who, knowingly and without lawful authority or reasonable excuse—

    (a) fails to comply with a notice under section 87(3) of this Act;

    (b) harbours or conceals a child—

        (i) as respects whom a parental responsibilities order has been made; and

        (ii) who has run away, or been taken away or whose return is required by such a notice; or

    (c) induces, assists or incites a child as respects whom any such order has been made to run away, or stay away, from a place where he is looked after or who takes away such a child from that place,

shall be guilty of an offence and liable, on summary conviction, to a fine not exceeding level 5 on the standard scale or to imprisonment for a term not exceeding six months or to both such fine and such imprisonment.

Offences in relation to parental responsibilities orders.

Miscellaneous

90. Nothing in this Part of this Act shall prejudice any capacity of a child enjoyed by virtue of section 2(4) of the Age of Legal Capacity (Scotland) Act 1991 (capacity of child with sufficient understanding to consent to surgical, medical or dental procedure or treatment); and without prejudice to that generality, where a condition contained, by virtue of—

    (a) section 66(4)(a), section 67(2) or section 69(9)(a) of this Act, in a warrant; or

    (b) section 70(5)(a) of this Act, in a supervision requirement,

requires a child to submit to any examination or treatment but the child has the capacity mentioned in the said section 2(4), the examination or treatment shall only be carried out if the child consents.

Consent of child to certain procedures.
1991 c.50.

91.—(1) All proceedings to which this section applies are civil proceedings for the purposes of section 32 of the Sheriff Courts (Scotland) Act 1971 (power of Court of Session to regulate civil procedure in the sheriff court).

(2) Any reference in this Part of this Act to regulation or prescription by rules in relation to any proceedings to which this section applies shall be construed, unless the context otherwise requires, as a reference to regulation or prescription by rules made under the said section 32.

(3) Without prejudice to the generality of the said section 32, rules may make provision as to—

    (a) the functions of a person appointed by the sheriff under section 41(1) of this Act and any right of that person to information relating to the proceedings;

    (b) the circumstances in which any person who has been given notice in accordance with such rules of an application for a child assessment order, or any other person specified in the rules, may apply to the court to have that order varied or discharged;

Procedural rules in relation to certain applications etc.
1971 c.58.

(c) the persons to whom notice of the making of a child protection order shall be given by the applicant for that order, and without prejudice to that generality may in making such provision require such notice to be given to either or both of the child and any relevant person in relation to that child;

(d) the persons to whom notice of an application for an exclusion order or, under section 79(3) of this Act, for the recall or variation of such an order or of anything done under section 77(2) of this Act shall be given;

(e) the period within which a hearing shall be held under subsection (5) of section 76 of this Act after the granting of an order under subsection (4) of that section;

(f) the service of any exclusion order on the named person and the appropriate person within such period as may be specified in the rules.

(4) In relation to any proceedings to which this section applies, rules may permit a party to such proceedings, in such circumstances as may be specified in the rules, to be represented by a person who is neither an advocate nor a solicitor.

(5) This section applies to any application made to the sheriff, and any other proceeding before the sheriff (whether on appeal or otherwise), under any provision of this Part of this Act.

Legal aid in respect of certain proceedings.
1986 c. 47.

92. For section 29 of the Legal Aid (Scotland) Act 1986 substitute the following section—

"Legal aid in respect of certain proceedings relating to children.

29.—(1) This section applies to legal aid in connection with—

(a) proceedings before the sheriff (including, without prejudice to that generality, proceedings on an appeal to the sheriff principal from a decision of the sheriff) in respect of any matter arising under Chapter 2 or 3 of Part II of the Children (Scotland) Act 1995 (in this section referred to as "the 1995 Act"); or

(b) an appeal to the Court of Session in connection with such proceedings.

(2) Subject to subsections (3) to (5) below, legal aid to which this section applies shall be available to a child and any relevant person in relation to him in connection with—

(a) proceedings before the sheriff on an application for a child protection order or child assessment order, or for the variation or recall of such an order;

(b) an appeal to the sheriff under section 51 of the 1995 Act against—

(i) a decision of a children's hearing to grant a warrant such as is mentioned in subsection (5)(a) of that subsection; or

(ii) any other decision of a children's hearing;

(c) an application—

(i) by virtue of section 65(7) or (9) of the 1995 Act for a finding as to whether the grounds for a referral are established; or

(ii) under section 85 of the 1995 Act for a review of such a finding;

(d) an appeal to the sheriff principal or to the Court of Session under section 51 of the 1995 Act.

(3) Legal aid shall be available under subsection (2)(b)(i) above on an application made to the sheriff without inquiry into the resources of the child or the relevant person.

(4) Legal aid shall be available under subsection (2)(a),(b)(ii) or (c) above on an application made to the sheriff if the sheriff is satisfied—

(a) that it is in the interests of the child that legal aid be made available; and

(b) after consideration of the financial circumstances of the child and any relevant person in relation to him that the expenses of the case cannot be met without undue hardship to the child or to any relevant person in relation to him or the dependants of any of them.

(5) Legal aid shall be available under subsection (2)(d) above on an application made to the Board if it is satisfied—

(a) after consideration of the financial circumstances of the child and any relevant person in relation to him that the expenses of the appeal cannot be met without undue hardship to the child or to any relevant person in relation to him or the dependants of any of them; and

(b) that the child, or as the case may be the relevant person, has substantial grounds for making or responding to the appeal and it is reasonable, in the particular circumstances of the case, that legal aid should be made available accordingly.

(6) The Board may require a person receiving legal aid under subsection (2)(d) above or subsection (9) below to comply with such conditions as it considers expedient to enable it to satisfy itself from time to time that it is reasonable for him to continue to receive such legal aid.

(7) Subject to subsection (8) below, legal aid to which this section applies shall be available in connection with proceedings before the sheriff on an application for an exclusion order (or for the variation or recall of such an order) to—

(a) a child;

(b) a relevant person in relation to a child;

(c) a person who is a named person, or will be such a person if the application is granted;

(d) a spouse or partner of a person mentioned in paragraph (c) above; and

(e) a person who is an appropriate person, or will be such a person if the application is granted.

(8) Legal aid shall be available under subsection (7) above on an application to the sheriff if the sheriff is satisfied after consideration of the financial circumstances of the applicant and, where the applicant is a child, of any relevant person or appropriate person in relation to him that the expenses of the case cannot be met without undue hardship to the applicant or any dependant of the applicant.

(9) Legal aid shall be available in connection with any appeal from a decision of the sheriff on an application for an exclusion order or for the variation or recall of such an order to any of the persons mentioned in paragraphs (a) to (e) of subsection (7) above on an application to the Board if it is satisfied—

(a) after consideration of the financial circumstances of the applicant and, where the applicant is a child, of any relevant person or appropriate person in relation to him, that the expenses of the appeal cannot be met without undue hardship to the applicant or any dependant of the applicant; and

(b) that the applicant has substantial grounds for making or responding to the appeal and that it is reasonable, in the particular circumstances of the case, that legal aid should be made available accordingly.

(10) Where in connection with any proceedings—

(a) the sheriff has been satisfied as is mentioned in subsection (4)(b) or subsection (8) above; or

(b) the Board has been satisfied as is mentioned in subsection (5)(a) or subsection (9)(a) above,

and has made legal aid available to any person, it shall not be necessary for the sheriff or, as the case may be, the Board to be so satisfied in respect of an application for legal aid by such a person in connection with any subsequent proceedings arising from such proceedings.

(11) Legal aid to which this section applies shall consist of representation by a solicitor and, where appropriate, by counsel in any proceedings (including any appeal) mentioned in subsection (1) above and shall include all such assistance as is usually given by solicitor or counsel in the steps preliminary or incidental to such proceedings.

(12) In this section—

(a) "child" and "relevant person" have the meanings given by section 93(2)(b) of the 1995 Act;

(b) "child protection order", "child assessment order" and "exclusion order" have the meanings given by section 93(1) of that Act;

(c) "named person" and "appropriate person" have the meanings given by section 76 of that Act; and

(d) "partner" shall be construed in accordance with section 79(4) of that Act.".

Interpretation of Part II

93.—(1) In this Part of this Act, unless the context otherwise requires,—

"accommodation" shall be construed in accordance with section 25(8) of this Act;

"chief social work officer" means an officer appointed under section 3 of the Social Work (Scotland) Act 1968;

"child assessment order" has the meaning given by section 55(1) of this Act;

"child protection order" has the meaning given by section 57(1) of this Act;

"children's hearing" shall be construed in accordance with section 39(3), but does not include a business meeting arranged under section 64, of this Act;

"compulsory measures of supervision" means, in respect of a child, such measures of supervision as may be imposed upon him by a children's hearing;

"constable" means a constable of a police force within the meaning of the Police (Scotland) Act 1967;

"contact order" has the meaning given by section 11(2)(d) of this Act;

"disabled" has the meaning given by section 23(2) of this Act;

"exclusion order" has the meaning given by section 76(12) of this Act;

"family", in relation to a child, includes—

(a) any person who has parental responsibility for the child; and

(b) any other person with whom the child has been living;

"local authority" means a council constituted under section 2 of the Local Government etc. (Scotland) Act 1994;

"local government area" shall be construed in accordance with section 1 of the said Act of 1994;

"parental responsibilities" has the meaning given by section 1(3) of this Act;

"parental responsibilities order" has the meaning given by section 86(1) of this Act;

"parental rights" has the meaning given by section 2(4) of this Act;

"place of safety", in relation to a child, means—

Interpretation of Part II.

1968 c. 49.

1967 c.77.

1994 c.39.

(a) a residential or other establishment provided by a local authority;

1989 c.41.

(b) a community home within the meaning of section 53 of the Children Act 1989;

(c) a police station; or

(d) a hospital, surgery or other suitable place, the occupier of which is willing temporarily to receive the child;

"the Principal Reporter" means the Principal Reporter appointed under section 127 of the said Act of 1994 or any officer of the Scottish Children's Reporter Administration to whom there is delegated, under section 131(1) of that Act, any function of the Principal Reporter under this Act;

"relevant local authority", in relation to a child who is subject to a warrant granted under this Part of this Act or to a supervision requirement, means the local authority for whose area the children's panel from which the children's hearing which granted the warrant or imposed the supervision requirement was formed;

"residence order" has the meaning given by section 11(2)(c) of this Act;

"residential establishment"—

(a) in relation to a place in Scotland, means an establishment (whether managed by a local authority, by a voluntary organisation or by any other person) which provides residential accommodation for children for the purposes of this Act or the Social Work (Scotland) Act 1968;

1968 c.49.

(b) in relation to a place in England and Wales, means a community home, voluntary home or registered children's home (within the meaning of the Children Act 1989); and

S.I. 1995/755 (N.I.2)

(c) in relation to a place in Northern Ireland, means a home provided under Part VIII of the Children (Northern Ireland) Order 1995, or a voluntary home, or a registered children's home (which have respectively the meanings given by that Order);

1980 c.44.

"school age" shall be construed in accordance with section 31 of the Education (Scotland) Act 1980;

"secure accommodation" means accommodation provided in a residential establishment, approved by the Secretary of State in accordance with regulations made under section 60(1)(bb) of the Social Work (Scotland) Act 1968 or under paragraph 4(2)(i) of Schedule 4 to the Children Act 1989, for the purpose of restricting the liberty of children;

"supervision requirement" has the meaning given by section 70(1) of this Act, and includes any condition contained in such a requirement or related to it;

"voluntary organisation" means a body (other than a public or local authority) whose activities are not carried on for profit; and

"working day" means every day except—

(a) Saturday and Sunday;

(b) December 25th and 26th; and

(c) January 1st and 2nd.

(2) For the purposes of—

(a) Chapter 1 and this Chapter (except this section) of this Part, "child" means a person under the age of eighteen years; and

(b) Chapters 2 and 3 of this Part—

"child" means—

(i) a child who has not attained the age of sixteen years;

(ii) a child over the age of sixteen years who has not attained the age of eighteen years and in respect of whom a supervision requirement is in force; or

(iii) a child whose case has been referred to a children's hearing by virtue of section 33 of this Act;

and for the purposes of the application of those Chapters to a person who has failed to attend school regularly without reasonable excuse includes a person who is over sixteen years of age but is not over school age; and

"relevant person" in relation to a child means—

(a) any parent enjoying parental responsibilities or parental rights under Part I of this Act;

(b) any person in whom parental responsibilities or rights are vested by, under or by virtue of this Act; and

(c) any person who appears to be a person who ordinarily (and other than by reason only of his employment) has charge of, or control over, the child.

(3) Where, in the course of any proceedings under Chapter 2 or 3 of this Part, a child ceases to be a child within the meaning of subsection (2) above, the provisions of those Chapters of this Part and of any statutory instrument made under those provisions shall continue to apply to him as if he had not so ceased to be a child.

(4) Any reference in this Part of this Act to a child—

(a) being "in need", is to his being in need of care and attention because—

(i) he is unlikely to achieve or maintain, or to have the opportunity of achieving or maintaining, a reasonable standard of health or development unless there are provided for him, under or by virtue of this Part, services by a local authority;

(ii) his health or development is likely significantly to be impaired, or further impaired, unless such services are so provided;

(iii) he is disabled; or

(iv) he is affected adversely by the disability of any other person in his family;

(b) who is "looked after" by a local authority, shall be construed in accordance with section 17(6) of this Act.

(5) Any reference to any proceedings under this Part of this Act, whether on an application or on appeal, being heard by the sheriff, shall be construed as a reference to such proceedings being heard by the sheriff in chambers.

PART III

ADOPTION

Approval of
adoption society
for specific
services.

94.—(1) In section 3 of the 1978 Act (approval of adoption societies)—

(a) for subsections (1) and (2) substitute—

"(1) Subject to any regulations made under section 9(1), a body which is a voluntary organisation may apply to the Secretary of State for his approval to its acting, or as the case may be continuing to act, as an adoption society, whether functioning generally or in relation to some service maintained, or to be maintained, as part of the Scottish Adoption Service and specified in the application (the service so specified being in this section and in section 4 referred to as the body's "specified service").

(1A) Application under subsection (1) shall be in such manner as may be specified in regulations made by the Secretary of State under this section.

(2) In considering an application under subsection (1), the Secretary of State shall take into account the matters relating to the applicant specified in subsections (3) to (5) and any other matters which appear to him to be relevant; and if, but only if, he is satisfied that, as the case may be, the applicant is likely to make, or is making, an effective contribution to the Scottish Adoption Service or to the applicant's specified service, he shall by notice to the applicant give the approval sought.

(2A) Approval under subsection (2) shall operate from such date as may be specified in the notice or, in the case of a renewal of approval, from the date of the notice.";

(b) in subsection (3)(a), the words ", including in particular its ability to make provision for children who are free for adoption" shall cease to have effect;

(c) in subsection (5), for the words "areas within which" substitute "geographical areas within which, the services as respects which";

(d) in subsection (6), after the word "Service" insert ", or as the case may be to the applicant's specified service"; and

(e) in subsection (7)—

(i) for the words "a period of" substitute "such period not exceeding"; and

(ii) after the word "operative" insert "as the Secretary of State may specify in the approval.".

(2) In section 4 of that Act (withdrawal of approval), after the word "Service" insert ", or as the case may be to the body's specified service,".

(3) In section 65(1) of that Act (interpretation), in the definition of "adoption society", after the word "for" insert ", or in connection with,".

95. For section 6 of the 1978 Act substitute—

"Duty to promote welfare of child.

6.—(1) Without prejudice to sections 12(8) and 18(8), in reaching any decision relating to the adoption of a child, a court or adoption agency shall have regard to all the circumstances but—

> (a) shall regard the need to safeguard and promote the welfare of the child concerned throughout his life as the paramount consideration; and
>
> (b) shall have regard so far as practicable—
>
>> (i) to his views (if he wishes to express them) taking account of his age and maturity; and
>>
>> (ii) to his religious persuasion, racial origin and cultural and linguistic background.

(2) Without prejudice to the generality of paragraph (b) of subsection (1), a child twelve years of age or more shall be presumed to be of sufficient age and maturity to form a view for the purposes of that paragraph.".

96. After section 6 of the 1978 Act there shall be inserted—

"Duty to consider alternatives to adoption.

6A. In complying with its duties under section 6 of this Act, an adoption agency shall, before making any arrangements for the adoption of a child, consider whether adoption is likely best to meet the needs of that child or whether for him there is some better, practicable, alternative; and if it concludes that there is such an alternative it shall not proceed to make those arrangements.".

97.—(1) In section 12 of the 1978 Act (making of adoption orders)—

(a) in subsection (3), at the beginning, insert "Subject to subsection (3A)"; and

(b) after subsection (3) insert—

"(3A) Where the adoption order is made by virtue of section 15(1)(aa), its making shall not operate to extinguish the parental responsibilities and parental rights which immediately before the making of the order were vested in the natural parent to whom the adopter is married.".

(2) In section 15(1) of that Act (adoption by one person)—

(a) after paragraph (a) insert—

"(aa) not being a person who may make application by virtue of paragraph (b) below, is married to a person—

> (i) who is the natural parent of the child concerned; and
>
> (ii) in whom are vested parental responsibilities and parental rights in relation to the child,"; and

(b) in paragraph (b), at the beginning insert—

> "not being a person who may make application by virtue of paragraph (aa) above,".

(3) In section 39 of that Act (status conferred by adoption), for subsection (1) substitute—

"(1) A child who is the subject of an adoption order shall be treated in law—

(a) where the adopters are a married couple, as if—

(i) he had been born as a legitimate child of the marriage (whether or not he was in fact born after the marriage was constituted); and

(ii) he were not the child of any person other than the adopters;

(b) where the adoption order is made by virtue of section 15(1)(aa) as if—

(i) he had been born as a legitimate child of the marriage between the adopter and the natural parent to whom the adopter is married (whether or not he was in fact born after the marriage was constituted); and

(ii) he were not the child of any person other than the adopter and that natural parent; and

(c) in any other case, as if—

(i) he had been born as a legitimate child of the adopter; and

(ii) he were not the child of any person other than the adopter.".

Further amendments of the 1978 Act; and interpretation of Part III.
1978 c. 28.

98.—(1) Schedule 2 to this Act, which contains further amendments of the 1978 Act, shall have effect.

(2) In this Part of this Act, "the 1978 Act" means the Adoption (Scotland) Act 1978.

PART IV

GENERAL AND SUPPLEMENTAL

Registration of births by persons who are themselves children.
1965 c. 49.
1991 c. 50.

99.—(1) In paragraph (a) of section 14(1) of the Registration of Births, Deaths and Marriages (Scotland) Act 1965 (duty of father and mother to give information of particulars of birth), for the words "father or mother of the child" substitute "child's father or mother (whether or not they have attained the age of sixteen years)".

(2) Where, at any time after the coming into force of the Age of Legal Capacity (Scotland) Act 1991 but before the coming into force of subsection (1) above, a person mentioned in the said paragraph (a) who had not at that time attained the age of sixteen years purported to fulfill the duty mentioned in the said section 14(1), he shall be presumed to have had legal capacity to fulfill that duty.

(3) In section 18 of the said Act of 1965 (registration of birth of child born out of wedlock), after subsection (2) add—

"(3) A person under the age of sixteen years has legal capacity—

(a) to make a request, declaration or statutory declaration under subsection (1) or (2)(b) above if, in the opinion of the registrar; or

(b) to make an application under subsection (2)(c) above if, in the opinion of the sheriff,

that person understands the nature of the request or, as the case may be, of the declaration, statutory declaration or application; and without prejudice to the generality of this subsection a person twelve years of age or more shall be presumed to be of sufficient age and maturity to have such understanding.".

(4) Where, at any time after the coming into force of the Age of Legal Capacity (Scotland) Act 1991 but before the coming into force of subsection (3) above, a person who had not at that time attained the age of sixteen years made a request, declaration, statutory declaration or application mentioned in subsection (1) or (2) of the said section 18 in relation to a child in respect of whose birth an entry was consequently made under the said subsection (1) in a register of births, or as the case may be under the said subsection (2) in the Register of Corrections etc., the person shall be presumed to have had legal capacity to make the request, declaration, statutory declaration, or application in question.

1991 c. 50.

100. After section 6A of the Social Work (Scotland) Act 1968 there shall be inserted—

Inquiries into matters affecting children.
1968 c. 49.

"Local authority inquiries into matters affecting children.

6B.—(1) Without prejudice to section 6A(1) of this Act, a local authority may cause an inquiry to be held into their functions under this Act, or any of the enactments mentioned in section 5(1B) of this Act, in so far as those functions relate to children.

(2) The local authority may, before an inquiry under this section is commenced, direct that it be held in private; but where no such direction is given, the person holding the inquiry may if he thinks fit hold it, or any part of it, in private.

(3) Subsections (2) to (6) of section 210 of the Local Government (Scotland) Act 1973 (powers in relation to local inquiries) shall apply in relation to an inquiry under this section as they apply in relation to a local inquiry under that section, so however that, for the purposes of the application, any reference in those subsections to a Minister shall be construed as a reference to the local authority and any reference to an officer of his Department as a reference to an officer of that authority.

1973 c. 45.

(4) The expenses incurred by a local authority in relation to an inquiry under this section (including such reasonable sum as the authority may determine for the services of any of their officers engaged in the inquiry) shall, unless the authority are of the opinion that those expenses should be defrayed in whole or in part by them, be paid by such party to the inquiry as they may direct; and the authority may certify the amount of the expenses so incurred.

(5) Any sum certified under subsection (4) above and to be defrayed in accordance with a direction under that subsection shall be a debt due by the party directed and shall be recoverable accordingly.

(6) The local authority may make an award as to the expenses of the parties at the inquiry and as to the parties by whom such expenses shall be paid.".

Panel for curators *ad litem*, reporting officers and safeguarders.
1978 c.28.

101.—(1) The Secretary of State may by regulations make provision for the establishment of a panel of persons from whom—

(a) curators *ad litem* may be appointed under section 58 of the Adoption (Scotland) Act 1978 or under section 87(4) of this Act;

(b) reporting officers may be appointed under those sections; and

(c) persons may be appointed under section 41(1) of this Act.

(2) Regulations under subsection (1) above may provide, without prejudice to the generality of that subsection—

(a) for the appointment, qualifications and training of persons who may be appointed to that panel; and

(b) for the management and organisation of persons available for appointment from that panel.

(3) Regulations under subsection (1) above may provide for the expenses incurred by persons appointed from the panel to be defrayed by a local authority.

Removal of duty to report on operation of Children Act 1975.
1975 c. 42.

102. Section 105 of the Children Act 1975 (which among other things provides that every five years there shall be laid before Parliament by the Secretary of State a report on the operation of such sections of that Act as are for the time being in force) shall cease to have effect.

Interpretation, rules, regulations and Parliamentary control.

103.—(1) Any reference in this Act, or in any enactment amended by this Act, to a person having, or to there being vested in him, parental responsibilities or parental rights shall, unless the context otherwise requires, be construed as a reference to his having, or to there being so vested, any of those rights or as the case may be responsibilities.

(2) Any reference in this Act to something being "prescribed" is, unless the context otherwise requires, a reference to its being prescribed by regulations; and any power conferred by this Act on the Secretary of State or the Lord Advocate to make rules or regulations shall be exercisable by statutory instrument which shall be subject to annulment in pursuance of a resolution of either House of Parliament.

(3) Rules or regulations made under this Act—

(a) may make different provision for different cases or classes of case; and

(b) may exclude certain cases or classes of case.

Financial provision.

104. There shall be paid out of money provided by Parliament—

(a) any expenses of the Secretary of State incurred in consequence of the provisions of this Act; and

(b) any increase attributable to this Act in the sums payable out of money so provided under any other enactment.

Extent, short title, minor and consequential amendments, repeals and commencement.

105.—(1) This Act, which subject to subsections (8) to (10) below extends to Scotland only—

(a) may be cited as the Children (Scotland) Act 1995; and

(b) except for subsections (1), (2) and (6) to (10) of this section, shall come into force on such day as the Secretary of State may by order made by statutory instrument appoint;

and different days may be appointed under paragraph (b) above for different purposes.

(2) An order under subsection (1)(b) above may contain such transitional and consequential provisions and savings as appear to the Secretary of State to be necessary or expedient in connection with the provisions brought into force.

(3) The transitional provisions and savings contained in Schedule 3 to this Act shall have effect but are without prejudice to sections 16 and 17 of the Interpretation Act 1978 (effect of repeals).

1978 c. 30.

(4) Schedule 4 to this Act, which contains minor amendments and amendments consequential upon the provisions of this Act, shall have effect.

(5) The enactments mentioned in Schedule 5 to this Act (which include spent provisions) are hereby repealed to the extent specified in the third column of that Schedule.

(6) The Secretary of State may by order made by statutory instrument make such further amendments or repeals, in such enactments as may be specified in the order, as appear to him to be necessary or expedient in consequence of any provision of this Act.

(7) A statutory instrument containing an order under subsection (6) above shall be subject to annulment in pursuance of a resolution of either House of Parliament.

(8) Sections 18, 26(2), 33, 44, 70(4), 74, 82, 83, 93 and 104 of this Act and this section extend to England and Wales, and those sections and this section (except section 70(4)) also extend to Northern Ireland; but—

(a) subsection (4) of this section so extends—

(i) to England and Wales, only in so far as it relates to paragraphs 8, 10, 19, 31, 37, 41(1), (2) and (7) to (9), 48 to 52, 54 and 55 of Schedule 4; and

(ii) to Northern Ireland, only in so far as it relates to paragraphs 31, 37, 41(1), (2) and (7) to (9), 54, 55 and 58 of that Schedule; and

(b) subsection (5) of this section so extends—

(i) to England and Wales, only in so far as it relates to the entries in Schedule 5 in respect of Part V of the Social Work (Scotland) Act 1968, the Maintenance Orders (Reciprocal Enforcement) Act 1972, section 35(4)(c) of the Family Law Act 1986, the Children Act 1989, the Child Support Act 1991 and the Education Act 1993; and

1968 c.49.
1972 c.18.
1986 c.55.
1989 c.41.
1991 c.48.
1993 c.35.

(ii) to Northern Ireland, only in so far as it relates to the entries in that Schedule in respect of Part V of the Social Work (Scotland) Act 1968, the Maintenance Orders (Reciprocal Enforcement) Act 1972 and section 35(4)(c) of the Family Law Act 1986.

(9) This section, so far as it relates to the repeal of Part V of the Social Work (Scotland) Act 1968, also extends to the Channel Islands.

(10) Her Majesty may by Order in Council direct that any of the relevant provisions specified in the Order shall extend, with such exceptions, adaptations and modifications (if any) as may be specified in the Order, to any of the Channel Islands; and in this subsection "the relevant provisions" means sections 74, 82, 83 and 93 of this Act and any regulations made under section 74 of this Act.

SCHEDULES

SCHEDULE 1

CHILDREN'S PANELS

Appointment

1. The Secretary of State shall, for each local government area, ap[...] number of members of children's panels as he considers appropriate[...] among that number appoint a chairman and a deputy chairman.

2. A member of a children's panel shall hold office for such period as is specified by the Secretary of State, but may be removed from office by the Secretary of State at any time.

Children's Panel Advisory Committees

3. Subject to paragraph 8 below, each local authority shall form a body (to be known as a "Children's Panel Advisory Committee") consisting of two members nominated by the local authority and three members nominated by the Secretary of State.

4. The Secretary of State may at the request of the local authority provide for an increase in the membership of the Children's Panel Advisory Committee appointed under paragraph 3 above by such number, not exceeding five, of additional members as the authority specify in relation to their request, the additional members to be nominated as follows—

   (a) the first, and any second or fourth additional member, by the Secretary of State;

   (b) any third or fifth additional member, by the local authority.

5. The chairman of the Children's Panel Advisory Committee shall be appointed by the Secretary of State from among such of the members he has nominated as are resident in the local government area for which the panel is appointed.

6. It shall be the duty of the Children's Panel Advisory Committee—

   (a) to submit names of possible panel members to the Secretary of State;

   (b) to advise the Secretary of State, in so far as he requires advice, on the suitability of persons referred to him as potential panel members; and

   (c) to advise the Secretary of State on such matters relating to the general administration of the panels as he may refer to them.

7. The Children's Panel Advisory Committee shall have power—

   (a) to appoint sub-committees;

   (b) to appoint to any such sub-committee a person who is not a member of the Children's Panel Advisory Committee; and

   (c) to refer all or any of the duties set out in paragraph 6 above to any such sub-committee for their advice.

Joint Advisory Committees

8.—(1) Two or more local authorities may, instead of each acting under paragraph 3 above, make arrangements to form a Children's Panel Advisory Committee for their areas (a "joint advisory committee").

(2) A joint advisory committee shall not be formed in pursuance of arrangements made under sub-paragraph (1) above unless the authorities concerned have obtained the consent in writing of the Secretary of State.

(3) The Secretary of State may give a direction, in any case where a joint advisory committee has not been formed, to two or more local authorities requiring them to form a joint advisory committee; and they shall comply with any such direction.

(4) Paragraphs 3 to 7, 10(a) and 11(b) of this Schedule shall apply to a joint advisory committee as they apply in respect of a Children's Panel Advisory Committee and, for the purposes of those paragraphs the local authorities acting under sub-paragraph (1) above shall be regarded as a single local authority.

Recruitment and training of panel members

9. The Secretary of State may make such arrangements as he considers appropriate to recruit and train members, or possible members, of the children's panels.

10. Each local authority shall make such arrangements as they consider appropriate—

(a) to enable the Children's Panel Advisory Committee to obtain names for submission to the Secretary of State as potential panel members; and

(b) to train panel members or potential panel members.

Expenses of panel members

11. A local authority may pay—

(a) to a member or a potential member of a children's panel,

(b) to a member of the Children's Panel Advisory Committee,

(c) to any person appointed under paragraph 7 above,

such allowances as may be determined by the Secretary of State; and he may determine differently in relation to different cases or different classes of case.

Publication of list of members of children's panel

12. Each local authority shall publish a list of names and addresses of members of the children's panel for their area, and that list shall be open for public inspection at the principal offices of the local authority, and at any place where an electors list for the local government area is available for inspection.

Section 98(1).

1978 c. 28.

SCHEDULE 2

AMENDMENTS OF THE ADOPTION (SCOTLAND) ACT 1978

1. The Adoption (Scotland) Act 1978 shall be amended in accordance with this Schedule.

2. In section 1(2) (facilities to be provided as part of adoption service)—

(a) paragraph (a) shall cease to have effect; and

(b) for paragraph (c) substitute—

"(bb) counselling and assistance (but, without prejudice to sections 51 to 51B, not assistance in cash) to children who have been adopted and to persons who have adopted a child; and

(c) counselling for other persons if they have problems relating to adoption.".

3. In section 3(3) (factors to be considered by Secretary of State in considering application for approval of adoption society), after paragraph (a) insert—

"(aa) the procedures in accordance with which the applicant deals with, or as the case may be proposes to deal with, complaints arising in relation to its exercise of its functions and, where the applicant is already an approved adoption society, the manner in which it deals with particular complaints,".

4. Section 8 (direction where adoption society inactive or defunct) shall cease to have effect.

5. In section 9 (regulations relating to an adoption agency's exercise of its functions)—

(a) in subsection (2), at the end add—

"including, without prejudice to the generality of this subsection, regulations as to procedures for dealing with complaints arising in relation to such exercise."; and

(b) after subsection (3) insert—

"(3A) Regulations under this section may make provision—

(a) as to the determination by an adoption agency of whether, as regards a child for whose adoption it proposes to make arrangements, any such agreement as is mentioned in sections 16(1)(b)(i) and 18(1)(a) is likely to be forthcoming and as to a period by the end of which, if they have determined that the agreement is unlikely to be forthcoming and if no application has been made for an adoption order in relation to the child, application for an order under section 18(1) shall require to be made in relation to him; and

(b) where the case of a child for whose adoption an adoption agency proposes to make arrangements is referred under section 73(4)(c)(ii) or (iii) of the Children (Scotland) Act 1995 to the Principal Reporter (within the meaning of Part II of that Act), as to circumstances in which and, on the occurrence of such circumstances, a period by the end of which, if no application has been made for an adoption order in relation to the child, application for an order under section 18(1) shall require to be made in relation to him.".

6. In section 11(3) (offence of receiving child illegally placed for adoption), for paragraph (c) substitute—

"(c) both receives a child placed with him in contravention of subsection (1) and knows that the placement is with a view to his adopting the child,".

7. In section 12 (adoption orders)—

(a) in subsection (1)—

(i) for the words "rights and duties relating" substitute "responsibilities and parental rights in relation"; and

(ii) at the end add—

"; except that an adoption order may be made in relation to a person who has attained the age of 18 years if the application for it was made before such attainment.";

(b) in subsection (2), for the words "rights and duties" substitute "responsibilities and parental rights";

(c) in subsection (3)—

(i) in paragraph (a), for the words "right or duty" substitute "responsibility or parental right"; and

(ii) in paragraph (b)(ii), for the words "rights and duties" substitute "responsibilities and parental rights"; and

(d) at the end add—

"(9) Where a court making an adoption order in relation to a child who is subject to a supervision requirement is satisfied that, in consequence of its doing so, compulsory measures of supervision in respect of the child are no longer necessary, it may determine that the child shall forthwith cease to be subject to that requirement.".

8. In section 14 (adoption by married couple)—

(a) in subsection (1), the words from "Subject" to "certain cases)" shall cease to have effect; and

(b) in subsection (2), after paragraph (b) add—

", or

(c) both of them were habitually resident in any of the places mentioned in paragraph (a) above throughout the period of one year which ends with the date of their application".

9. In section 15 (adoption by one person)—

(a) in subsection (1), the words from "Subject" to "certain cases)" shall cease to have effect; and

(b) in subsection (2), after paragraph (b) add—

", or

(c) he was habitually resident in any of the places mentioned in paragraph (a) above throughout the period of one year which ends with the date of his application".

10. In section 16 (provision for parental agreement to adoption order)—

(a) for subsection (2) substitute—

"(2) The grounds mentioned in subsection (1)(b)(ii) are, that the parent or guardian—

(a) is not known, cannot be found or is incapable of giving agreement;

(b) is withholding agreement unreasonably;

(c) has persistently failed, without reasonable cause, to fulfil one or other of the following parental responsibilities in relation to the child—

(i) the responsibility to safeguard and promote the child's health, development and welfare; or

(ii) if the child is not living with him, the responsibility to maintain personal relations and direct contact with the child on a regular basis;

(d) has seriously ill-treated the child, whose reintegration into the same household as the parent or guardian is, because of the serious ill-treatment or for other reasons, unlikely."; and

(b) subsection (5) shall cease to have effect.

11. In section 18 (making and effect of orders freeing for adoption)—

(a) in subsection (1), after the word "agency" insert "which is a local authority";

(b) for subsection (5) substitute—

"(5) On the making of an order under this section, the parental responsibilities and parental rights in relation to the child are transferred to the adoption agency.";

(c) for subsection (7) substitute—

"(7) Before making an order under this section in the case of a child whose father is not, and has not been, married to the mother and does not have any parental responsibilities or parental rights in relation to the child, the court shall satisfy itself in relation to any person claiming to be the father that—

(a) he has no intention of applying for, or, if he did so apply, it is likely that he would be refused, an order under section 11 of the Children (Scotland) Act 1995 (orders in relation to parental responsibilities and parental rights); and

(b) he has no intention of entering into an agreement with the mother under section 4(1) of that Act (acquisition by natural father by agreement of such responsibilities and rights), or, if he has such an intention, that no agreement under that subsection is likely to be made."; and

(d) at the end add—

"(9) Where a court making an order under this section in relation to a child who is subject to a supervision requirement is satisfied that, in consequence of its doing so, compulsory measures of supervision in respect of the child are no longer necessary, it may determine that the child shall forthwith cease to be subject to that requirement.".

12. In section 19 (progress reports)—

(a) in subsection (1)—

(i) for the words "("the former parent")" substitute "(in this section and in section 20 referred to as the "relevant parent")"; and

(ii) for the words "did not do so" substitute—

"either—

(a) did not do so; or

(b) having done so, subsequently by written notice under this subsection to the adoption agency to which the parental responsibilities and parental rights have been transferred, has withdrawn such declaration.";

(b) in subsection (2)—

(i) for the words "in which the parental rights and duties were vested" substitute "to which the parental responsibilities and parental rights were transferred"; and

(ii) for the word "former", in both places where it occurs, substitute "relevant";

(c) in subsection (3)—

(i) for the word "former", wherever it occurs, substitute "relevant"; and

(ii) for the words "have his home with a person with whom he has been placed for adoption" substitute "be placed with a person with a view to his being adopted by that person"; and

(d) in subsection (4)—

(i) for the words "the former" substitute "the relevant";

(ii) after paragraph (b) add—

"but a declaration under this subsection may be withdrawn in the same way as may a declaration under subsection (6) of section 18, in which event the agency shall no longer be so released"; and

(iii) for the words "that former" substitute "that relevant".

13. In section 20 (revocation of order under section 18)—

(a) in subsection (1)—

(i) for the word "former" substitute "relevant"; and

(ii) for the words "rights and duties" substitute "responsibilities and parental rights";

(b) after subsection (1) insert—

"(1A) The adoption agency, at any time after the making of the order under section 18 when the conditions mentioned in paragraphs (a) and (b) of subsection (1) above are satisfied, may apply to the court which made the order for a further order revoking it.";

(c) in subsection (2)—

(i) for the words "the application" substitute "an application under subsection (1) or (1A)"; and

(ii) for the words "rights and duties" substitute "responsibilities and parental rights";

(d) for subsection (3) substitute—

"(3) Where an order freeing a child for adoption is revoked under this section, the court shall, by an order under section 11 of the Children (Scotland) Act 1995 determine on whom are to be imposed the parental responsibilities, and to whom are to be given the parental rights, in relation to the child.";

(e) in subsection (4)—

(i) for the words "if the application" substitute "if an application under subsection (1)"; and

(ii) in paragraph (a), for the word "former" substitute "relevant"; and

(f) in subsection (5), for the word "former" substitute "relevant".

14. In section 21 (variation of order under section 18 so as to substitute one adoption agency for another)—

(a) in subsection (1)—

(i) for the words "rights and duties" substitute "responsibilities and parental rights"; and

(ii) for the words "in which they are vested under" substitute "to which they are transferred by virtue of"; and

(b) in subsection (3)—

(i) for the words "rights and duties" substitute "responsibilities and parental rights"; and

(ii) for the words "vested in" substitute "been transferred to".

15. After section 22 insert—

"Children subject to supervision requirements.

22A.—(1) An approved adoption society shall refer the case of a child who is subject to a supervision requirement to the Principal Reporter where it is satisfied that the best interests of the child would be served by its placing the child for adoption and it intends so to place him.

(2) On a case being referred to him under subsection (1), the Principal Reporter shall arrange for a children's hearing to review the supervision requirement in question and shall make any arrangements incidental to that review.

(3) Subsections (9), (13) and (14) of section 73 of the Children (Scotland) Act 1995 (which provide, respectively, for acting on the review of a supervision requirement, a report by a children's hearing and consideration of that report) shall apply in relation to a children's hearing arranged under this section as those subsections apply in relation to one arranged by virtue of subsection (4)(c)(iii) of that section.

(4) In this section "Principal Reporter" has the same meaning as in Part II of the Children (Scotland) Act 1995.".

16. In section 24 (restrictions on making adoption orders), for subsection (2) substitute—

"(2) The court may make an adoption order in relation to a child even where it is found that the applicants have, as respects the child, contravened section 51.

(3) In considering whether to make an adoption order or an order under section 18(1), the court shall regard the welfare of the child concerned as its paramount consideration and shall not make the order in question unless it considers that it would be better for the child that it should do so than that it should not.".

17. In section 25(1) (making of interim order and preconditions for so doing)—

(a) for the words "of sections 16(1) and 22(1) are complied with" substitute—

"—

(a) of section 16(1); and

(b) in a case where the child was not placed with the applicant by an adoption agency, of section 22(1),

are complied with"; and

(b) for the words "vesting the custody of the child in" substitute "giving parental responsibilities and parental rights to".

18. After section 25 insert—

"Timetable for resolving question as to whether agreement to adoption order etc. should be dispensed with.

25A. In proceedings in which the question arises as to whether the court is satisfied as is mentioned in section 16(1)(b)(ii) or 18(1)(b), the court shall, with a view to determining the question without delay—

(a) draw up a timetable specifying periods within which certain steps must be taken in relation to those proceedings; and

(b) give such directions as it considers appropriate for the purpose of ensuring, so far as is reasonably practicable, that the timetable is adhered to.".

19. In section 27 (restrictions on removal of a child by a parent or guardian who has agreed to an adoption order or to an order freeing the child for adoption)—

    (a) for subsections (1) and (2), substitute—

        "(1) Where—

            (a) an adoption agency has placed a child with a person with a view to his being adopted by the person; and

            (b) the consent of each parent or guardian of the child has been duly obtained to that placement (whether or not in knowledge of the identity of the person),

        any such parent or guardian shall not be entitled to remove the child from the care and possession of the person without the leave either of the adoption agency or of the court.

        (2) The reference in subsection (1) to consent having been duly obtained is to its having been obtained in accordance with such regulations as may be made by the Secretary of State for the purposes of this section."; and

    (b) in subsection (3), for the words "contravenes subsection (1) or (2)" substitute "removes a child in contravention of subsection (1)".

20. In section 28 (restriction on removal of child from care and possession of applicant for adoption order etc.)—

    (a) in subsection (4), for the words from ", in terms of" to the end substitute "under or by virtue of Chapter 2 or 3 of Part II of the Children (Scotland) Act 1995"; and

    (b) in subsection (5), the words "or of a voluntary organisation" and "or the organisation" shall cease to have effect.

21. Sections 32 to 37 (protected children) shall cease to have effect.

22. In section 45(5) (restrictions as to persons to whom information contained in the Adopted Children Register or in certain other registers or books may be provided, including a restriction as to the minimum age which an adopted person must be for it to be provided to him), for the word "17" substitute "16".

23. In section 49(1) (adoption of children abroad), for the words "vesting in him the parental rights and duties relating" substitute "transferring to him the parental responsibilities and parental rights in relation".

24. In section 51 (prohibition on certain payments)—

    (a) in subsection (1), after the word "section" insert "and of section 51A(3)";

    (b) in subsection (2), for the words "the court may order any child in respect of whom the offence was committed" substitute "without prejudice to any power which the court has to make any other order in relation to the child as respects whom the offence was committed, it may order him";

    (c) in subsection (5)—

        (i) at the beginning insert "Subject to section 51B,"; and

        (ii) at the end add "(including any such payment made by virtue of section 51B)"; and

    (d) subsections (6)(a) and (7) to (11) shall cease to have effect.

25. After section 51 insert—

"Adoption
allowances
schemes.

51A.—(1) Subject to subsection (2), an adoption agency which is—

(a) a local authority shall, within such period after the coming into force of this section as the Secretary of State may by order direct;

(b) an approved adoption society may,

prepare a scheme (in this section and in section 51B referred to as an "adoption allowances scheme") for the payment by the agency of allowances to any person who has adopted, or intends to adopt, a child in any case where arrangements for the adoption were made, or as the case may be are to be made, by the agency.

(2) The Secretary of State may make regulations as respects adoption allowances schemes; and without prejudice to the generality of this subsection such regulations may in particular make provision as to—

(a) the procedure to be followed by an agency in determining whether a person should be paid an allowance;

(b) the circumstances in which an allowance may be paid;

(c) the factors to be taken into account in determining the amount of an allowance;

(d) the procedure for review, variation and termination of allowances;

(e) the information about allowances which is to be supplied by an agency to a person who intends to adopt a child; and

(f) the procedure to be followed by an agency in drawing up, in making alterations to, or in revoking and replacing, an adoption allowances scheme.

(3) Section 51(1) shall not apply to any payment made in accordance with an adoption allowances scheme (including any such payment made by virtue of section 51B).

Transitional
provisions as
respects adoption
allowances.

51B. After the coming into force of section 51A—

(a) no scheme for the payment of allowances shall be submissible under subsection (5) of section 51; and

(b) a scheme which has been approved under that subsection of that section shall forthwith be revoked under subsection (6)(b) of that section, so however that where a person was before its revocation receiving payments made in accordance with that scheme he may continue to receive payments so made which, had there been no revocation, would have fallen to be made to him or he may agree to receive, instead of the continued payments, payments made in accordance with an adoption allowances scheme.".

26. In section 58 (curators *ad litem* and reporting officers), in subsection (2)(c), for the words "rights and duties relating" substitute "responsibilities and parental rights in relation".

27. In section 59(4) (disapplication of provisions regarding rules), for the words ", 11 and 32 to 37" substitute "and 11".

28. In section 60(3) (affirmative procedure for certain orders), the words "or 51(9)" shall cease to have effect.

29. In section 65 (interpretation)—

(a) in subsection (1)—

(i) in the definition of "adoption order", in each of paragraphs (b) and (c), for the words "and 30 to 32" substitute "30 and 31";

(ii) after the definition of "child" insert—

""compulsory measures of supervision" has the same meaning as in Part II of the Children (Scotland) Act 1995;";

(iii) in the definition of "guardian", paragraph (b) shall cease to have effect;

(iv) in the definition of "local authority", the words ", 35(1)" shall cease to have effect;

(v) after the definition of "overseas adoption" insert—

""parent" means, irrespective of whether or not they are, or have been, married to each other—

(a) the mother of the child, where she has parental responsibilities or parental rights in relation to him;

(b) the father of the child where he has such responsibilities or rights; and

(c) both of his parents, where both have such responsibilities or rights;

"parental responsibilities" and "parental rights" have the meanings respectively given by sections 1(3) and 2(4) of the Children (Scotland) Act 1995 (analogous expressions being construed accordingly);";

(vi) in the definition of "relative" for the words from "and any person" to the end substitute "where he is not a parent within the meaning of this Act, and any person who would be a relative within the meaning of this definition if the father were such a parent;" and

(vii) after the definition of "specified order" insert—

""supervision requirement" has the same meaning as in Part II of the Children (Scotland) Act 1995;";

(b) in subsection (3), for the words "44 of the Social Work (Scotland) Act 1968" substitute "70 of the Children (Scotland) Act 1995"; and

(c) after subsection (5) add—

"(6) Any reference in this Act to a child being in, received into or kept in, care (whether or not such care is expressed as being the care of a local authority and except where the context otherwise requires) shall be taken to be a reference to his being looked after by a local authority and shall be construed in accordance with section 17(6) of the Children (Scotland) Act 1995; and any reference to the authority in whose care a child is, shall be construed accordingly.".

SCHEDULE 3

TRANSITIONAL PROVISIONS AND SAVINGS

1. Where, immediately before the day appointed for the coming into force of section 25 of this Act, a child is by virtue of section 15 of the 1968 Act (duty of local authority to provide for orphans, deserted children etc.) in the care of a local authority, the child shall on and after that day be treated as if he had been provided with accommodation under (and within the meaning of) subsection (1) of the said section 25.

2. Sections 29 and 30 of this Act shall apply in respect of a person who, at the time when he ceased to be of school age (as defined in section 31 of the Education (Scotland) Act 1980) or at any subsequent time, was—

1980 c. 44.

   (a) in the care of a local authority by virtue of the said section 15 or of section 16 of the 1968 Act (assumption of parental rights and powers); or

   (b) subject to a supervision requirement (within the meaning of section 44(1) of the 1968 Act),

as they apply in respect of a person who at such time was looked after (within the meaning of Part II of this Act) by a local authority.

3. Where the parental rights in respect of a child have, by a resolution under the said section 16 or under section 16A of the 1968 Act (duty of local authority in cases of necessity to assume parental rights and powers vested in a voluntary organisation), vested in a local authority and immediately before the day appointed for the coming into force of section 86 of this Act those rights remain so vested, the resolution shall on and after that day have effect as if it were a parental responsibilities order transferring the appropriate parental rights and responsibilities (as defined in subsection (3) of the said section 86) relating to the child to the authority; and any access order made under section 17B of the 1968 Act in relation to the child (with any order made under section 17C of that Act as respects the access order) being (in either case) an order which immediately before that day remains undischarged, shall on and after that day have effect as if it were an order made under section 88(3) of this Act as respects the child.

4. Where the parental rights in respect of a child have, by a resolution under the said section 16, vested in a voluntary organisation (as defined in section 93 of this Act) and immediately before the day mentioned in paragraph 3 above those rights remain so vested, the resolution shall, notwithstanding the repeal by this Act of the said section 16, continue to have effect until one of the following occurs—

   (a) the child attains the age of eighteen years;

   (b) the resolution is rescinded by the local authority because it appears to them that their doing so would promote the child's welfare;

   (c) the period of six months commencing with that day expires;

   (d) an order is made by virtue of section 11(2)(b), or under section 86(1), of this Act in relation to the child;

   (e) an order is made under section 12 (adoption order) or 18 (order freeing for adoption) of the Adoption (Scotland) Act 1978 in relation to the child.

1978 c. 21.

5. Where the circumstance by virtue of which a resolution under the said section 16 ceases to have effect is that mentioned in sub-paragraph (c) of paragraph 4 above, the appropriate parental rights and responsibilities (defined as mentioned in paragraph 3 above) in relation to the child shall transfer forthwith to the local authority in whose area he resides; and for the purposes of sections 86(6) and 87 to 89 of this Act the transfer shall be deemed effected by a parental responsibilities order applied for by that authority.

6. While a resolution continues to have effect by virtue of paragraph 4 above, sections 17(3A) and (6) to (10), 17A, 17B, 17D, 17E and 20(3) of the 1968 Act

(together with the code of practice last published under subsection (5) of the said section 17E) shall continue to have effect in relation to the child in question notwithstanding the repeal by this Act of those sections.

7. Where an order made under—

    (a) section 10 (power of court in actions of divorce etc. to commit care of child to local authority) or 12 (power of court to provide for supervision of child) of the Matrimonial Proceedings (Children) Act 1958;

    (b) section 11 of the Guardianship Act 1973 (orders relating to care and custody of children); or

    (c) section 26 of the Adoption (Scotland) Act 1978 (provision for supervision or care where adoption order refused),

committed the care of the child to, or as the case may be placed the child under the supervision of, a local authority and immediately before the repeal by this Act of the section in question (the "relevant repeal") that order remained undischarged, the order shall continue to have effect notwithstanding the relevant repeal until one of the following occurs—

    (i) the period of six months commencing with the date of the relevant repeal expires;

    (ii) the Court of Session direct, or the sheriff directs, that the order be discharged; or

    (iii) there is an event in consequence of which, but for the provisions (apart from this paragraph) of this Act, the order would have fallen to be discharged.

8.—(1) Where relevant proceedings in relation to a child have been commenced and on the relevant date have not been concluded, the provisions of Part III of the 1968 Act shall continue to apply to those proceedings until the proceedings are concluded, notwithstanding the repeal of any of those provisions by this Act.

(2) For the purposes of this paragraph, "relevant proceedings" means any proceedings at a children's hearing under Part III of the 1968 Act, any application to the sheriff under that Part for a warrant or under section 42(2)(c) of that Act to establish any ground of referral, and any appeal under section 49 or 50 of that Act; and a reference to the commencement, or to the conclusion, of such proceedings shall be construed in accordance with sub-paragraph (3) or, as the case may be, (4) below.

(3) Relevant proceedings are commenced when one of the following occurs—

    (a) a children's hearing is arranged under section 37(4) or section 39(3) of the 1968 Act;

    (b) an application under section 42(2)(c) of that Act is lodged;

    (c) an appeal to the sheriff under section 49 of that Act is lodged;

    (d) an application under section 50(2) of that Act is made.

(4) Relevant proceedings are concluded when one of the following occurs—

    (a) the sheriff discharges the referral under section 42(5) of the 1968 Act;

    (b) a children's hearing discharge the referral under section 43(2) of that Act;

    (c) the period of three weeks after a children's hearing make a supervision requirement under section 44 of that Act or on remission to them under section 49(5) of that Act, expires provided that no appeal has been lodged within that period against that decision under section 49 of that Act;

1958 c. 40.

1973 c. 29.

1978 c. 21.

(d) subject, as respects a decision under section 49(5)(b) of that Act, to head (c) above, the period of twenty eight days after the sheriff has disposed of an appeal under section 49(4), (5) or (6) of that Act expires provided that no application has been made within that period to him to state a case under section 50(2) of that Act;

(e) the period of twenty eight days after the sheriff has disposed of a case remitted to him under section 50(3) expires provided that no further application under the said section 50(2) has been made.

9. Where a child has been taken to a place of safety, or is being detained in such a place, in accordance with section 37(2) of the 1968 Act before the relevant date, and the first lawful day for the purposes of subsection (4) of that section is on or after that date, the child's case shall be proceeded with as if that day had been before the relevant date.

10.—(1) Where on the relevant date a child is subject to a supervision requirement imposed under section 44 of the 1968 Act, he shall be treated as if the requirement had been imposed under section 70 of this Act; and in calculating any period of time for the purposes of section 73 of this Act, that requirement shall be deemed to have been imposed on the day on which the requirement was imposed under the said section 44 or, as the case may be, was last reviewed or varied under the said Act of 1968.

(2) Where any relevant proceedings are concluded as mentioned in paragraph 8(4)(c) above, a supervision requirement imposed under section 44 of the 1968 Act shall have effect as if it were made under section 70 of this Act.

(3) Where before the relevant date, or in any relevant proceedings, the sheriff has in relation to a supervision requirement made an order under section 49(6) of the 1968 Act, that order shall have effect in relation to the supervision requirement deemed to have been made under section 70 of this Act as it would have had effect in relation to the supervision requirement made under section 44 of the 1968 Act.

11. In this Schedule—

"the 1968 Act" means the Social Work (Scotland) Act 1968;   1968 c. 49.

"the relevant date" means the date on which the repeal of Part III of the 1968 Act by this Act takes effect; and

"relevant proceedings" shall be construed in accordance with paragraph 8(2) above.

SCHEDULE 4   Section 105(4).

MINOR AND CONSEQUENTIAL AMENDMENTS

Lands Clauses Consolidation (Scotland) Act 1845 (c.19)

1.—(1) The Lands Clauses Consolidation (Scotland) Act 1845 shall be amended in accordance with this paragraph.

(2) In section 7 (which makes provision for certain persons to have full power to sell and convey land)—

(a) after the word "husbands," insert "persons who, within the meaning of Part I of the Children (Scotland) Act 1995, are entitled to act as the legal representatives of a child,";

(b) after the words "guardians for" the words "persons under a legal disability by reason of nonage" shall cease to have effect; and

(c) after the word "whether", the words "persons under legal disability by reason of nonage" shall cease to have effect;

(d) after the word "such" where it appears for the sixth time, insert "legal representatives,"; and

(e) after the word "such" where it appears for the seventh time, the words "persons under legal disability by reason of nonage" shall cease to have effect.

(3) In section 67 (certain payments to persons under a disability to be deposited with the Bank)—

(a) after the word "husband," insert "a person who, within the meaning of Part I of the Children (Scotland) Act 1995, is entitled to act as a legal representative of a child"; and

(b) the words "persons under legal disability by reason of nonage" shall cease to have effect.

(4) In section 69 (nomination of trustees to whom certain payments of under £200 may be paid)—

(a) the words "legal disability by reason of nonage" shall cease to have effect; and

(b) after the word "husbands," insert "legal representatives of a child (within the meaning of Part I of the Children (Scotland) Act 1995),".

(5) In section 70 (sums of under £20 to be paid to certain persons), after the word "husbands," insert "legal representatives of a child (within the meaning of Part I of the Children (Scotland) Act 1995),".

Judicial Factors (Scotland) Act 1849 (c.51)

2.—(1) The Judicial Factors (Scotland) Act 1849 shall be amended in accordance with this paragraph.

(2) In section 1 (interpretation), the words from "the word "Guardian"" to "years;" shall cease to have effect.

(3) In section 10 (duty of accountant to supervise judicial factors and others), for the words "guardians and tutors" substitute ", tutors".

(4) Section 25(2) (guardians to be subject to the provisions of the Act), shall cease to have effect.

(5) In section 27 (limitation by court of amount of caution), the words "guardians and" shall cease to have effect.

(6) In section 31 (power of court to remove tutors etc.), the word "guardian" shall cease to have effect.

(7) In section 32 (provisions of the Act not to alter existing powers, rights and duties of offices), the word "guardian," shall cease to have effect.

(8) In section 33 (power of accountant to obtain information from banks), the words "guardians or" shall cease to have effect.

(9) In section 34 (petitions for discharge of office), in both places where it occurs, the word "guardian," shall cease to have effect.

(10) In section 34A (act of sederunt to provide for other forms of discharge), for the words ", death or coming of age" substitute "or death".

(11) In section 36 (records held by accountant to be open to inspection), the word "guardianships," shall cease to have effect.

(12) In section 37 (accumulation of interest on accounts), the word "guardian," shall cease to have effect.

(13) In section 40 (act of sederunt to regulate *inter alia* application of the Act to offices other than judicial factors), in both places where it occurs, the word "guardians," shall cease to have effect.

Improvement of Land Act 1864 (c.114)

3. In section 24 of the Improvement of Land Act 1864 (representation of persons under disability in certain applications etc.), for the words from the beginning to "feoffee" where it last occurs substitute "Any person entitled to act as the legal representative of a person under legal disability by reason of non age or mental incapacity shall be entitled to act on behalf of that person for the purposes of this Act; and any trustee, judicial factor, executor or administrator shall, subject to any other enactment, have the same rights and powers for the purposes of this Act as if the property vested in or administered by him had been vested in him in his own right; but no such legal representative".

Judicial Factors (Scotland) Act 1880 (c.4)

4. In section 3 of the Judicial Factors (Scotland) Act 1880 (interpretation), in the definition of "judicial factor"—

(a) for the word "*absentis*," substitute "*absentis* and"; and

(b) the words from "and" to "required," shall cease to have effect.

Heritable Securities (Scotland) Act 1894 (c.44)

5. In section 13 of the Heritable Securities (Scotland) Act 1894 (persons to have powers conferred by Act where person subject to legal disability), for the words "and trustees" substitute "and—

(a) any person entitled, within the meaning of Part I of the Children (Scotland) Act 1995, to act as the legal representative of a child; and

(b) trustees".

Trusts (Scotland) Act 1921 (c.58)

6. In section 2 of the Trusts (Scotland) Act 1921 (interpretation)—

(a) in the definition of "trustee", the words "(including a father or mother acting as guardian of a child under the age of 16 years)" shall cease to have effect; and

(b) after the definition of "trustee" insert—

""curator" and "tutor" shall have respectively the meanings assigned to these expressions by section 1 of the Judicial Factors Act 1849;

"guardian" shall not include any person who, within the meaning of Part I of the Children (Scotland) Act 1995, is entitled to act as the legal representative of a child;".

Children and Young Persons (Scotland) Act 1937 (c. 37)

7.—(1) The Children and Young Persons (Scotland) Act 1937 shall be amended in accordance with this paragraph.

(2) In section 12 (cruelty to persons under sixteen)—

(a) in subsection (1), for the words from "has the custody" to "that age" substitute "who has parental responsibilities in relation to a child or to a young person under that age or has charge or care of a child or such a young person,";

(b) in subsection (2)(a), after the words "young person" insert "or the legal guardian of a child or young person"; and

(c) in subsection (4), for the words from "of whom" to "or care" substitute

"and he had parental responsibilities in relation to, or charge or care of, that child or young person".

(3) In section 15 (causing or allowing persons under sixteen to be used for begging), in each of subsections (1) and (2), for the words "the custody" substitute "parental responsibilities in relation to, or having".

(4) In section 22 (exposing children under seven to risk of burning), for the words from "having the custody" to "seven years" substitute "and who has parental responsibilities in relation to a child under the age of seven years or charge or care of such a child".

(5) In section 27 (interpretation)—

(a) the first paragraph shall cease to have effect; and

(b) in the second paragraph, for the words "the custody of" substitute "parental responsibilities in relation to".

(6) In section 110(1) (interpretation)—

(a) after the definition of "local authority" insert—

""parental responsibilities" has the same meaning as in section 1(3) of the Children (Scotland) Act 1995 and includes the responsibilities which a father would have as a parent but for the operation of section 3(1)(b) of that Act;";

(b) for the definition of "place of safety", substitute ""place of safety" has the meaning give by section 93(1) of the Children (Scotland) Act 1995;"; and

(c) for the definition of "residential establishment" substitute ""residential establishment" has the meaning given by the said section 93(1);".

Mines and Quarries Act 1954 (c. 70)

8. In section 182(1) of the Mines and Quarries Act 1954 (interpretation), in the definition of "parent", for the words from "means" to "and includes" substitute "means a parent of a young person or any person who is not a parent of his but who has parental responsibility for him (within the meaning of the Children Act 1989) or who has parental responsibilities in relation to him (within the meaning of section 1(3) of the Children (Scotland) Act 1995), and includes".

1989 c. 41.

Matrimonial Proceedings (Children) Act 1958 (c. 40)

9. In section 11(1) of the Matrimonial Proceedings (Children) Act 1958 (reports as to arrangements for future care and upbringing of children), for the words from the beginning to "the court may" substitute "Where the court is considering any question relating to the care and upbringing of a child, it may".

Factories Act 1961 (c. 34)

10. In section 176(1) of the Factories Act 1961 (interpretation)—

(a) for the definition of "child" substitute—

""child" means any person who is not over—

(a) compulsory school age (construed in accordance with section 277 of the Education Act 1993); or

1993 c. 35.

(b) school age (construed in accordance with section 31 of the Education (Scotland) Act 1980);"

1980 c. 44.

(b) in the definition of "parent", for the words from "means" to "and includes" substitute "means a parent of a child or young person or any person who is not a parent of his but who has parental responsibility for him (within the meaning of the Children Act 1989) or who has parental responsibilities in relation to him (within the meaning of section 1(3) of the Children (Scotland) Act 1995), and includes".

Education (Scotland) Act 1962 (c. 47)

11. In section 145(33) of the Education (Scotland) Act 1962 (interpretation), for the words "the actual custody of" substitute "parental responsibilities (within the meaning of section 1(3) of the Children (Scotland) Act 1995) in relation to, or has the care of,".

Registration of Births, Deaths and Marriages (Scotland) Act 1965 (c. 49)

12.—(1) The Registration of Births, Deaths and Marriages (Scotland) Act 1965 shall be amended in accordance with this paragraph.

(2) In section 20(3)(a) (re-registration of birth of person under sixteen), for sub-paragraphs (i) and (ii) substitute ", by any person (whether or not he has himself attained the age of sixteen years) having parental responsibilities in relation to that person;".

(3) In section 43 (recording of baptismal name or change of name or surname)—

    (a) in subsection (3), the words from "In this" to the end shall cease to have effect;

    (b) in subsections (6)(a) and (7), for the words "the parent or guardian" substitute "the qualified applicant";

    (c) after subsection (9) insert—

      "(9A) In this section "qualified applicant" means—

        (a) where only one parent has parental responsibilities in relation to the child, that parent;

        (b) where both parents have such responsibilities in relation to the child, both parents; and

        (c) where neither parent has such responsibilities, any other person who has such responsibilities.

      (9B) A person may be a qualified applicant for the purposes of this section whether or not he has attained the age of sixteen years"; and

    (d) subsection (10) shall cease to have effect.

(4) In section 53(3)(c) (offence of failure by parent to give information concerning birth), after the word "fails" insert "without reasonable excuse".

(5) In section 56(1) (interpretation), after the definition of "parentage" insert—

    ""parental responsibilities" has the meaning given in section 1(3) of the Children (Scotland) Act 1995;"

13. Where, at any time after the coming into force of the Age of Legal Capacity (Scotland) Act 1991 but before the coming into force of—   1991 c. 50.

    (a) sub-paragraph (2) of paragraph 12 of this Schedule, a person's mother or father, who had not at that time attained the age of sixteen years, purported to apply under section 20(3)(a) of that Act to re-register the person's birth, the mother, or as the case may be the father, shall be presumed to have had legal capacity to make the application; or

    (b) sub-paragraph (3)(c) of that paragraph, a person who had not at that time attained the age of sixteen years purported to make an application under any provision of section 43 of that Act ("making an application" including for the purposes of this sub-paragraph, without prejudice to the generality of that expression, signing and delivering a certificate in accordance with subsection (3) of that section) the person shall be presumed to have had legal capacity to make the application.

Law Reform (Miscellaneous Provisions)(Scotland) Act 1966 (c.19)

14. In section 8 of the Law Reform (Miscellaneous Provisions)(Scotland) Act 1966 (variation and recall of certain orders in respect of maintenance, custody etc.)—

    (a) in subsection (1), after paragraph (c) insert—

        "(cc) an order under section 11 of the Children (Scotland) Act 1995 (orders in respect of parental responsibilities etc.) or under any earlier enactment relating to the custody, care or supervision of a child, or access to a child;"; and

    (b) in subsection (6), in the definition of "sheriff", in paragraph (a), for the words "or (c)" substitute ", (c) or (cc)".

Social Work (Scotland) Act 1968 (c.49)

15.—(1) The Social Work (Scotland) Act 1968 shall be amended in accordance with this paragraph.

(2) In section 1(1) (duty of local authority to implement statutory duties not falling on other authorities), after the word "Act" insert "or Part II of the Children (Scotland) Act 1995".

(3) In section 4 (arrangements for provision of assistance to local authorities by other bodies), after "1984" insert "or Part II of the Children (Scotland) Act 1995".

(4) In section 5 (powers of the Secretary of State in relation to certain functions of local authorities)—

    (a) in subsection (1) after the word "Act" insert "and Part II of the Children (Scotland) Act 1995";

    (b) in subsection (1B)—

        (i) before paragraph (o), the word "and" shall cease to have effect; and

        (ii) at the end add "; and

    (p) Part II of the Children (Scotland) Act 1995.";

    (c) in subsection (2), in paragraph (c) for the words "and (o)" substitute ", (o) and (p)"; and

    (d) for subsection (3) substitute—

    "(3) Without prejudice to the generality of subsection (2) above, regulations under this section may make such provision as is mentioned in subsection (4) of this section as regards—

        (a) the boarding out of persons other than children by local authorities and voluntary organisations, whether under any enactment or otherwise; and

        (b) the placing of children under paragraph (a), or the making of arrangements in respect of children under paragraph (c), of section 26(1) of the Children (Scotland) Act 1995, by local authorities.

    (4) The provision referred to in subsection (3) of this section is—

        (a) for the recording—

            (i) by local authorities and voluntary organisations, of information relating to those with whom persons are so boarded out, or who are willing to have persons so boarded out with them; and

(ii) by local authorities, of information relating to those with whom children are so placed or with whom such arrangements are made or who are willing to have children so placed with them or to enter into such arrangements;

(b) for securing that—

(i) persons are not so boarded out in any household unless it is for the time being approved by such local authority or voluntary organisation as may be prescribed by the regulations; and

(ii) children are not so placed or, in accordance with such arrangements, provided with accommodation, in any household unless it is for the time being approved by the local authority placing the child or as the case may be making the arrangements;

(c) for securing that, where possible, the person with whom a child is so placed or with whom such arrangements are made is either of the same religious persuasion as the child or gives an undertaking that the child shall be brought up in that persuasion;

(d) for securing—

(i) that a person who is, and the place in which he is, so boarded out by a local authority or voluntary organisation is supervised and inspected by that authority or organisation; and

(ii) that a child who is, and the place in which he is, so placed or, in accordance with such arrangements, provided with accommodation, by a local authority is supervised and inspected by that authority,

and that he shall be removed from the place in question if his welfare appears to require it.

(5) In subsections (3) and (4) of this section, "child" has the same meaning as in Chapters 2 and 3 of Part II of the Children (Scotland) Act 1995."

(5) In section 5B (requirement to establish complaints procedures)—

(a) in subsection (4), in paragraph (b), for the words "rights in respect of" substitute "responsibilities and parental rights (within the meaning of section 1(3) and section 2(4) respectively of the Children (Scotland) Act 1995) in relation to"; and

(b) in subsection (5), at the end of the definition of "child", the words from "and" to the end of the subsection shall cease to have effect.

(6) In section 6 (power to enter certain establishments to conduct examination)—

(a) in subsection (1)—

(i) in paragraph (a), after the word "1984" insert "or Part II of the Children (Scotland) Act 1995";

(ii) in paragraph (b), sub-paragraph (ii) shall cease to have effect;

(iii) in paragraph (c), after the word "person" insert ", other than a child,"; and

(iv) after paragraph (c) add—

"(cc) any place where a child is for the time being accommodated under paragraph (a) of, or by virtue of paragraph (c) of, section 26(1) of the Children (Scotland) Act 1995."; and

(b) in subsection (2), after the words "1984" insert "or Part II of the Children (Scotland) Act 1995".

(7) For subsection (1) of section 6A (power of the Secretary of State to hold inquiries), substitute—

"(1) Without prejudice to section 6B(1) of this Act, the Secretary of State may cause an inquiry to be held into—

(a) the functions of a local authority under this Act or any of the enactments mentioned in section 5(1B) of this Act;

(b) the functions of an adoption society, within the meaning of section 65 of the Adoption (Scotland) Act 1978;

1978 c.28.

(c) the functions of a voluntary organisation in so far as those functions relate to establishments to which sections 61 to 68 of this Act apply;

(d) the detention of a child under—

1937 c.37.

(i) section 57 of the Children and Young Persons (Scotland) Act 1937; or

1975 c.21.

(ii) section 206 or 413 of the Criminal Procedure (Scotland) Act 1975; or

1994 c.39.

(e) the functions of the Principal Reporter under Part III of the Local Government (Scotland) Act 1994, the Children (Scotland) Act 1995 or any other enactment."

(8) In section 9 (powers of the Secretary of State with regard to training etc.), in subsections (1) and (2), after the word "Act" insert "or Part II of the Children (Scotland) Act 1995".

(9) In section 10(1) (making of grants and loans for social work), for the words "and (l)" substitute ", (l) and (p)".

(10) In section 11(1) (local authority authorised by Secretary of State to purchase compulsorily land), in subsection (1), after the word "Act" insert "or Part II of the Children (Scotland) Act 1995".

(11) In section 12 (general social welfare services of local authorities), for the words from "be given" in subsection (1) to "a person" in subsection (2)(b) substitute—

", subject to subsections (3) to (5) of this section, be given in kind or in cash to, or in respect of, any relevant person.

(2) A person is a relevant person for the purposes of this section if, not being less than eighteen years of age, he is".

(12) In section 28 (burial or cremation)—

(a) in subsection (1), after the word "from," insert "or was a child being looked after by,"; and

(b) after subsection (2) add—

"(3) In subsection (1) of this section, the reference to a child being looked after by a local authority shall be construed in accordance with section 17(6) of the Children (Scotland) Act 1995.".

(13) In section 29 (power of local authority to defray expenses of parents etc. visiting persons accommodated by a local authority or attending certain funerals)—

(a) in subsection (1)—

(i) for the words from "a person" to "respect" substitute—

"—

(a) a person, other than a child, in the care of the authority or receiving assistance from the authority; or

(b) a child who is being looked after by the authority,

in respect";

(ii) after the words "visiting the person" insert "or child"; and

(iii) for the words "the person", where they occur for the second time, substitute "him";

(b) in subsection (2), for the words from "a person" to "for" substitute—

"—

(a) a person, other than a child, who had been in the care of the authority or receiving assistance from the authority; or

(b) a child who had been looked after by the authority,

for"; and

(c) after subsection (2), add—

"(3) In subsections (1) and (2) above, references to a child looked after by a local authority shall be construed as is mentioned in subsection (3) of section 28 of this Act.".

(14) Part III (children in need of compulsory measures of care) shall cease to have effect, with the exception of subsections (1) and (3) of section 31 and the amendments provided for by the said subsection (3) and contained in Schedule 2 to that Act.

(15) In section 59(1) (provision and maintenance of residential and other establishments) after the word "Act,", where it occurs for the second time, insert "or under Part II of the Children (Scotland) Act 1995,

(16) In section 68 (visiting of persons in establishments)—

(a) in subsection (2), for the words "in the care or under the supervision of the authority under Part II or Part III of this Act" substitute "being looked after by the authority"; and

(b) after subsection (3) add—

"(4) In subsection (2) of this section, the reference to children being looked after by a local authority shall be construed in accordance with section 17(6) of the Children (Scotland) Act 1995.".

(17) In section 78 (duty to make contributions in respect of children in care etc.)—

(a) in subsection (1)—

(i) for the words "has been received into care under Part II of this Act" substitute "is being looked after by a local authority"; and

(ii) in paragraph (a), for the words "his father and mother" substitute "any natural person who has parental responsibilities (within the meaning of section 1(3) of the Children (Scotland) Act 1995) in relation to him"; and

(b) for subsection (2) substitute—

"(2) This Part of this Act applies to any supervision requirement which, under paragraph (a) of section 70(3) of the Children (Scotland) Act 1995, requires the child concerned to reside in a place or places other than his own home.".

(18) In section 78A (recovery of contributions), in subsection (2)(a), for the words "in their care or under their supervision" substitute "looked after by them".

(19) In section 79 (recipients of contributions)—

(a) in subsection (1), for the words "in the care or under the supervision of" substitute "looked after by"; and

(b) in subsection (2), for the words "having the care or supervision of" substitute "looking after".

(20) In section 80 (enforcement of duty to make contributions)—

(a) in subsection (1), for the words from "received" to "requirement" substitute "looked after by a local authority";

(b) in subsection (4), for paragraphs (a) and (b) substitute "throughout the period during which he is looked after by a local authority";

(c) in subsection (5), for the words "is the maintainable child's father or mother" substitute ", being a natural person, has parental responsibilities (within the meaning of section 1(3) of the Children (Scotland) Act 1995) in relation to the maintainable child"; and

(d) in subsection (7), for the words "having the care or supervision of" substitute "looking after".

(21) In section 82(1) (recovery of arrears of contributions), for the words "having the care or supervision of" substitute "looking after".

(22) In section 83(2) (variation of trusts where person in whose care a child has been residing is for the time being residing in England, Wales or Northern Ireland), for the words "having the care or supervision of" substitute "looking after".

(23) After section 83 insert—

"References in this Part of this Act to child being looked after.

83A. In this Part of this Act, references to a child being looked after by a local authority shall be construed in accordance with section 17(6) of the Children (Scotland) Act 1995.".

(24) In section 86 (adjustments between local authorities as regards certain expenditure)—

(a) in subsection (1)—

(i) in paragraph (a), after the word "Act" insert ", or under section 25 of the Children (Scotland) Act 1995,"; and

(ii) in paragraph (b), for the words from "of services" to "Act", where it occurs for the second time, substitute ", or under or by virtue of Part II of the said Act of 1995, of services and facilities for a person ordinarily so resident (including, in the case of a child, any expenses incurred after he has ceased to be a child, and, in the event of another local authority taking over, under section 25(4) of that Act, the provision of accommodation for him,"; and

(b) in subsection (3), after the words "1989" insert "or provided with accommodation under paragraph (a) of, or by virtue of paragraph (c) of, section 26(1) of the Children (Scotland) Act 1995".

(25) In section 87 (charges which may be made for services and accommodation), in each of subsections (1) and (1A), after the words "1984" there shall be inserted "or under or by virtue of Part II of the Children (Scotland) Act 1995".

(26) Section 88 (duty of parents to notify change of address) shall cease to have effect.

(27) In section 90(1) (power to make regulations, orders or rules), the words "(other than orders under section 52 and 58 and Part V of this Act)" shall cease to have effect.

(28) In section 94(1) (interpretation)—

(a) the definition of "children's panel" and of "children's hearing" shall cease to have effect;

(b) the definition of "compulsory measures of care" shall cease to have effect;

    (c) in the definition of "establishment", after the word "Act," insert "or of Part II of the Children (Scotland) Act 1995,";

    (d) the definition of "guardian" shall cease to have effect;

    (e) for the definition of "parent" substitute—

    ""parent" means either parent or both parents, except that where the child was born out of wedlock and the parents have not subsequently married each other it means the natural mother but not the natural father;";

    (f) the definition of "place of safety" shall cease to have effect;

    (g) in the definition of "prescribed"—

        (i) in paragraph (a), for the words "sections 3 and 36" substitute "section 3"; and

        (ii) paragraph (b) shall cease to have effect;

    (h) in the definition of "residential establishment", after the word "Act" insert "or of Part II of the Children (Scotland) Act 1995";

    (i) the definition of "school age" shall cease to have effect;

    (j) in the definition of "supervision requirement", for the words "section 44(1) of this Act" substitute "section 70(1) of the Children (Scotland) Act 1995"; and

    (k) for the definition of "training school" substitute—

    ""training school" has the meaning assigned to it by section 180(1) of the Children and Young Persons Act (Northern Ireland) 1968;".

(29) In section 97 (provisions of the Act which extend to England and Wales)—

    (a) in subsection (1), the words "section 44(1) (except head (b)) and (1A)", "section 58" and "Part V" shall cease to have effect; and

    (b) subsections (2) and (3) shall cease to have effect.

(30) In Schedule 2 (general adaptations of Part IV of Children and Young Persons (Scotland) Act 1937), for paragraph 1 substitute—   1937 c. 37.

"1. Any reference to a child or to a young person shall be construed as a reference to a child as defined in section 93(2)(b) of the Children (Scotland) Act 1995.".

Children and Young Persons Act 1969 (c. 54)

16. In Schedule 5 to the Children and Young Persons Act 1969, paragraphs 57 and 65(1) (which relate to the provision of accommodation for children outside Scotland) shall cease to have effect.

Chronically Sick and Disabled Persons Act 1970 (c. 44)

17.—(1) The Chronically Sick and Disabled Persons Act 1970 shall be amended in accordance with this paragraph.

(2) In section 18(2) (information as to accommodation of younger with older persons), for the words "having functions under the Social Work (Scotland) Act 1968" substitute ", in respect of their functions both under the Social Work (Scotland) Act 1968 and under the Children (Scotland) Act 1995,".

(3) In section 29(2) (modifications of provisions of the Act in their application to Scotland)—

    (a) in paragraph (a), at the end add "except that in the case of persons under eighteen years of age such references shall instead be construed as references to duties to disabled children (within the meaning of Chapter 1 of Part II of the Children (Scotland) Act 1995)"; and

(b) for paragraph (b) substitute—

"(b) any references to services provided under arrangements made by a local authority under the said section 29 shall be construed as references to services for—

(i) such chronically sick or disabled, or such mentally disordered, persons provided by virtue of the said section 12; or

(ii) such disabled children provided under section 23(1) of the said Act of 1995,

by a local authority;".

Sheriff Courts (Scotland) Act 1971 (c. 58)

18.—(1) The Sheriff Courts (Scotland) Act 1971 shall be amended in accordance with this paragraph.

(2) In section 32(1) (power of Court of Session to regulate civil procedure in the sheriff court), after paragraph (i) insert—

"(j) permitting a person who is not an advocate or solicitor and is not represented by an advocate or solicitor to transmit, whether orally or in writing, the views of a child to the sheriff for the purposes of any enactment which makes provision (however expressed) for the sheriff to have regard to those views;".

(3) In section 37(2A) (remit to Court of Session), for the words "the custody" substitute "parental responsibilities or parental rights (within the meaning of sections 1(3) and 2(4) respectively of the Children (Scotland) Act 1995) in relation to a child or the".

Employment of Children Act 1973 (c. 24)

19. In section 2(2A) of the Employment of Children Act 1973 (supervision by education authorities), for paragraph (b) substitute—

"(b) in Scotland, if he has parental responsibilities (within the meaning of section 1(3) of the Children (Scotland) Act 1995) in relation to the child or care of him.".

Domicile and Matrimonial Proceedings Act 1973 (c. 45)

20.—(1) The Domicile and Matrimonial Proceedings Act 1973 shall be amended in accordance with this paragraph.

(2) In section 10 (ancillary and collateral orders)—

(a) in subsection (1)—

(i) for the words from the beginning to "in connection with" substitute "Where after the commencement of this Act an application is competently made to the Court of Session or to a sheriff court for the making, or the variation or recall, of an order which is ancillary or collateral to";

(ii) the words "as respects the person or property in question" shall cease to have effect; and

(b) after subsection (1) insert—

"(1A) For the purposes of subsection (1) above, references to an application for the making, or the variation or recall, of an order are references to the making, or the variation or recall, of an order relating to children, aliment, financial provision on divorce, judicial separation, nullity of marriage or expenses.".

(3) In paragraph 11 of Schedule 3 (sisting of consistorial action)—

(a) in sub-paragraph (1), in the definition of "the relevant order", for the words from "made" to the end substitute "relating to aliment or children"; and

(b) in sub-paragraph (3), for the words "custody of a child, and the education of a child" substitute "arrangements to be made as to with whom a child is to live, contact with a child, and any other matter relating to parental responsibilities within the meaning of section 1(3) of the Children (Scotland) Act 1995 or parental rights within the meaning of section 2(4) of that Act".

Land Compensation (Scotland) Act 1973 (c. 56)

21.—(1) The Land Compensation (Scotland) Act 1973 shall be amended in accordance with this paragraph.

(2) In section 35(3) (disturbance payments where modification of dwelling required for disabled person), in paragraph (a), after "1968" insert "or section 23 of the Children (Scotland) Act 1995".

(3) In section 80(1) (interpretation), in the definition of "disabled person"—

(a) after "means" insert "—

(a)"; and

(b) after "1972" insert "; and

(b) a child in need within the meaning of section 93(4)(a)(iii) of the Children (Scotland) Act 1995".

Local Government (Scotland) Act 1973 (c. 65)

22.—(1) The Local Government (Scotland) Act 1973 shall be amended in accordance with this paragraph.

(2) In section 56(9) (enactments exempted from repeal by virtue of that section), for paragraph (d) substitute—

"(d) paragraphs 3 and 8 of Schedule 1 to the Children (Scotland) Act 1995 (Children's Panel Advisory Committees and joint advisory committees);".

(3) In Schedule 25, paragraph 41 shall cease to have effect.

(4) In Schedule 27, paragraphs 185 and 187 shall cease to have effect.

Rehabilitation of Offenders Act 1974 (c. 53)

23.—(1) The Rehabilitation of Offenders Act 1974 shall be amended in accordance with this paragraph.

(2) In section 3 (special provision with respect to certain disposals by children's hearings)—

(a) for the words "Social Work (Scotland) Act 1968 is that mentioned in section 32(2)(g)" substitute "Children (Scotland) Act 1995 is that mentioned in section 52(2)(i)"; and

(b) for the words "to the satisfaction of the sheriff under section 42 of that Act, the acceptance or establishment" substitute "(or deemed established) to the satisfaction of the sheriff under section 68 or 85 of that Act, the acceptance, establishment (or deemed establishment)".

(3) In section 5 (rehabilitation periods for particular sentences)—

(a) in subsection (3)(b), for the words "43(2) of the Social Work (Scotland) Act 1968" substitute "69(1)(b) and (12) of the Children (Scotland) Act 1995";

(b) in subsection (5)(f), for the words "Social Work (Scotland) Act 1968" substitute "Children (Scotland) Act 1995";

(c) in subsection (10), for the words "Social Work (Scotland) Act 1968" substitute "Children (Scotland) Act 1995"; and

(d) subsection (10A) shall cease to have effect.

(4) In section 7(2) (limitations on rehabilitation)—

    (a) for paragraph (c) substitute—

        "(c) in any proceedings relating to parental responsibilities or parental rights (within the meaning of section 1(3) and section 2(4) respectively of the Children (Scotland) Act 1995), guardianship, adoption or the provision by any person of accommodation, care or schooling for children under the age of 18 years;

            (cc) in any proceedings under Part II of the Children (Scotland) Act 1995;";

    (b) paragraph (e) shall cease to have effect; and

    (c) the words from "In the application" to the end shall cease to have effect.

Criminal Procedure (Scotland) Act 1975 (c. 21)

24.—(1) The Criminal Procedure (Scotland) Act 1975 shall be amended in accordance with this paragraph.

(2) Section 14 shall cease to have effect.

1995 c. 20.

(3) In section 23 (which, as amended by the Criminal Justice (Scotland) Act 1995, provides for remand of persons under twenty-one in secure accommodation)—

1968 c. 49.

    (a) in sub-paragraph (i) of paragraph (a) of subsection (1), for the words "the Social Work (Scotland) Act 1968" substitute "Part II of the Children (Scotland) Act 1995"; and

    (b) in paragraph (a) of subsection (4), for the words "the Social Work (Scotland) Act 1968" substitute "Part II of the Children (Scotland) Act 1995".

(4) In section 37 (power to order parent to give security for child's good behaviour) after subsection (3) add—

    "(4) In this section "parent" means either of the child's parents, if that parent has parental responsibilities or parental rights (within the meaning of sections 1(3) and 2(4) respectively of the Children (Scotland) Act 1995) in relation to him.".

(5) In section 39 (attendance at court of parent of child charged with an offence: solemn procedure)—

    (a) for subsection (4) substitute—

    "(4) The parent or guardian whose attendance shall be required under this section shall be—

        (a) any parent who has parental responsibilities or parental rights (within the meaning of sections 1(3) and 2(4) respectively of the Children (Scotland) Act 1995) in relation to the child; or

        (b) the guardian having actual possession and control of him."; and

    (b) in subsection (5), for the word "custody" substitute "care".

(6) In section 168 (power of court to refer child to reporter where accused convicted of certain offences: solemn proceedings)—

    (a) in paragraph (c), the word "female" shall cease to have effect;

(b) in paragraph (ii), after the word "above" insert "or the person in respect of whom the offence so mentioned was committed"; and

(c) for the words "Part III of the Social Work (Scotland) Act 1968" substitute "Chapter 3 of Part II of the Children (Scotland) Act 1995".

1968 c. 49.

(7) In section 171(2) (regard to be had to certain provisions in presumption of age of child: solemn proceedings)—

(a) for the words "application of the provisions of section 30(1) of the Social Work (Scotland) Act 1968" substitute "definition of a child for the purposes of Chapters 2 and 3 of Part II of the Children (Scotland) Act 1995"; and

(b) for the words "under Part V of that Act" substitute "by virtue of regulations made under that Act for the purpose of giving effect to orders made in different parts of the United Kingdom".

(8) In section 177 (directions by court in solemn proceedings as to conveyance of person to residential establishment), the words "provided by a local authority under Part IV of the Social Work (Scotland) Act 1968" shall cease to have effect".

(9) In section 296 (powers of police in relation to children apprehended)—

(a) in subsection (3), the words from "and the child" to the end shall cease to have effect; and

(b) subsection (4) shall cease to have effect.

(10) In section 304 (power to require parent to give security for child's good behaviour), after subsection (3) add—

"(4) In this section "parent" means either of the child's parents, if that parent has parental responsibilities or parental rights (within the meaning of sections 1(3) and 2(4) respectively of the Children (Scotland) Act 1995) in relation to him.".

(11) In section 307 (attendance at court of parent of child charged with an offence: summary procedure)—

(a) for subsection (4) substitute—

"(4) The parent or guardian whose attendance shall be required under this section shall be—

(a) any parent who has parental responsibilities or parental rights (within the meaning of sections 1(3) and 2(4) respectively of the Children (Scotland) Act 1995) in relation to the child; or

(b) the guardian having actual possession and control of him."; and

(b) in subsection (5), for the word "custody" substitute "care".

(12) Section 323 shall cease to have effect.

(13) In section 329 (which, as amended by the Criminal Justice (Scotland) Act 1995, provides for remand of persons under twenty-one in secure accommodation)—

1995 c. 20.

(a) in sub-paragraph (i) of paragraph (a) of subsection (1), for the words "the Social Work (Scotland) Act 1968" substitute "Part II of the Children (Scotland) Act 1995"; and

(b) in paragraph (a) of subsection (4), for the words "the Social Work (Scotland) Act 1968" substitute "Part II of the Children (Scotland) Act 1995".

(14) In section 364 (power of court to refer child to reporter where accused convicted of certain offences: summary proceedings)—

(a) in paragraph (c), the word "female" shall cease to have effect;

(b) in paragraph (ii), after the word "above" insert "or the person in respect of whom the offence so mentioned was committed"; and

(c) for the words "Part III of the Social Work (Scotland) Act 1968" substitute "Chapter 3 of Part II of the Children (Scotland) Act 1995".

(15) In section 368(2) (regard to be had to certain provisions in presumption of age of child: summary proceedings)—

(a) for the words "application of the provisions of section 30(1) of the Social Work (Scotland) Act 1968" substitute "definition of a child for the purposes of Chapters 2 and 3 of Part II of the Children (Scotland) Act 1995"; and

(b) for the words "under Part V of that Act" substitute "by virtue of regulations made under that Act for the purpose of giving effect to orders made in different parts of the United Kingdom".

(16) In section 378 (directions by court in summary proceedings as to conveyance of person to residential establishment), the words "provided by a local authority under Part IV of the Social Work (Scotland) Act 1968" shall cease to have effect.

(17) In section 413 (detention of children found guilty in summary proceedings)—

(a) in subsection (1), for the words "residential care" substitute "residential accommodation provided under Part II of the Children (Scotland) Act 1995";

(b) in subsection (3)—

(i) the definitions of "care" and of "the 1968 Act" shall cease to have effect; and

(ii) after the definition of "the appropriate local authority" insert—

"secure accommodation" has the meaning assigned to it in Part II of the Children (Scotland) Act 1995";

(c) after subsection (3) insert the following subsection—

"(3A) Where a child in respect of whom an order is made under this section is detained by the appropriate local authority, that authority shall have the same powers and duties in respect of the child as they would have if he were subject to a supervision requirement.";

(d) in subsection (4), the words "within the meaning of the 1968 Act" shall cease to have effect;

(e) in subsection (5), the words "(within the meaning of the 1968 Act)" shall cease to have effect;

(f) in subsection (6), for the word "care" substitute "accommodation";

(g) in subsection (6A), the words "within the meaning of the 1968 Act" shall cease to have effect;

(h) in subsection (6B)—

(i) for the words "care of" substitute "accommodation provided by"; and

(ii) for the words "their care" substitute "that accommodation or any other such accommodation provided by that authority"; and

(i) in subsection (6C)—

(i) for the word "care", 'where it first occurs', substitute "accommodation provided by the appropriate local authority";

(ii) in paragraph (a), for the word "care" substitute "accommodation"; and

(iii) in paragraph (b), for the words "residential care" where they first occur substitute "detention in residential accommodation" and for those words where they secondly occur substitute "such detention".

(18) In section 462 (interpretation) in the definition of—

(a) "child", for the words "by section 30 of the Social Work (Scotland) Act 1968" substitute "for the purposes of Chapters 2 and 3 of Part II of the Children (Scotland) Act 1995";

1968 c. 49.

(b) "children's hearing", for the words "by section 34(1) of the Social Work (Scotland) Act 1968" substitute "in Part II of the Children (Scotland) Act 1995";

(c) "place of safety", for the words "section 94(1) of the Social Work (Scotland) Act 1968" substitute "Part II of the Children (Scotland) Act 1995";

(d) "residential establishment", for the words from "has" to the end substitute "means an establishment within the meaning of that expression for the purposes of the Social Work (Scotland) Act 1968 or, as the case may be, of Part II of the Children (Scotland) Act 1995"; and

(e) "supervision requirement", for the words "by section 44(1) of the Social Work (Scotland) Act 1968" substitute "in Part II of the Children (Scotland) Act 1995".

Local Government (Scotland) Act 1975 (c. 30)

25. In section 23(2) of the Local Government (Scotland) Act 1975 (bodies subject to investigation by Commissioner for Local Administration in Scotland), for paragraph (d) substitute—

"(d) any Children's Panel Advisory Committee formed under paragraph 3, or joint advisory committee formed under paragraph 8, of Schedule 1 to the Children (Scotland) Act 1995;".

Children Act 1975 (c. 72)

26.—(1) The Children Act 1975 shall be amended in accordance with this paragraph.

(2) Sections 47 to 49 shall cease to have effect.

(3) In section 50 (payments towards maintenance for children), for the words from "custody" to "authority" substitute "a child under the age of sixteen is residing with and being cared for (other than as a foster child) by a person other than a parent of the child, a council constituted under section 2 of the Local Government (Scotland) Act 1994".

1994 c. 39.

(4) In section 51 (restriction on removal of child where applicant has provided home for three years)—

(a) in subsection (1), for the words "custody of" substitute "a residence order in relation to";

(b) for subsection (2) substitute—

"(2) In any case where subsection (1) applies, and the child—

(a) was being looked after by a council constituted under section 2 of the Local Government etc. (Scotland) Act 1994 before he began to have his home with the applicant, and

(b) continues to be looked after by such a council,

the council by whom the child is being looked after shall not remove him from the applicant's care and possession except—

(i) with the applicant's consent;

    (ii) with the leave of the court; or

    (iii) in accordance with an order made, or authority or warrant granted, under Chapter 2 or 3 of Part II of the Children (Scotland) Act 1995."; and

(c) at the end add—

    "(5) In this section "looked after" and "residence order" have the meanings given respectively by section 17(6) and section 11(2)(c) of the Children (Scotland) Act 1995; and "residence order" shall have the same meaning in sections 52 and 53 of this Act.".

    (5) In section 52 (return of child taken away in breach of section 51), for the words "custody of" substitute "a residence order in relation to".

    (6) Section 53 (custody order on application for adoption in Scotland) shall cease to have effect.

    (7) In section 55 (interpretation and extent), for the words "sections 47 to 54", in both places where they occur, substitute "sections 50 to 53".

    (8) Sections 73 to 84, 89, 99, 100, 102 and 103 shall cease to have effect.

    (9) Section 107 (interpretation), except in so far as subsection (1) defines "adoption society", "child" and "voluntary organisation", shall cease to have effect.

    (10) In Schedule 3 (minor and consequential amendments), paragraphs 52 to 57 shall cease to have effect.

Sexual Offences (Scotland) Act 1976 (c. 67)

    27.—(1) The Sexual Offences (Scotland) Act 1976 shall be amended in accordance with this paragraph.

    (2) In section 11(1) (causing or encouraging seduction, prostitution etc. of girls under sixteen), for the words "the custody" substitute "parental responsibilities (within the meaning of section 1(3) of the Children (Scotland) Act 1995), in relation to, or having".

    (3) In section 14(1) (allowing child to be in brothel), for the words "the custody" substitute "parental responsibilities (within the meaning of section 1(3) of the Children (Scotland) Act 1995), in relation to, or having".

Education (Scotland) Act 1980 (c. 44)

    28.—(1) The Education (Scotland) Act 1980 shall be amended in accordance with this paragraph.

    (2) In section 36(3) (referral to reporter of case of irregular school attendance), for the words from "may" to the end substitute ", where no requirement arises under section 53(1) of the Children (Scotland) Act 1995 to give information about the child to the Principal Reporter, may under this subsection provide the Principal Reporter with such information.".

    (3) In section 44—

    (a) subsection (1) (referral by court to Principal Reporter of case involving offence against section 35) shall cease to have effect; and

    (b) in subsection (2) (powers of court where no referral to Principal Reporter), for the words "subsection (1) above, make a direction" substitute "section 54(1) of the Children (Scotland) Act 1995, refer the matter to the Principal Reporter".

(4) In section 65B(6) (sending of report in relation to recorded child)—

(a) paragraph (a) shall cease to have effect; and

(b) at the end add—

"and the local authority as education authority shall also ensure that the local authority for the purposes of Part II of the Children (Scotland) Act 1995 receive such a copy.".

(5) In section 135(1) (interpretation)—

(a) in the definition of "parent", for the words "the actual custody of" substitute "parental responsibilities (within the meaning of section 1(3) of the Children (Scotland) Act 1995) in relation to, or has care of";

(b) the definition of "reporter of the appropriate local authority" shall cease to have effect;

(c) for the definition of "residential establishment" substitute—

""residential establishment" has the meaning given by paragraph (a) of the definition of that expression in section 93(1) of the Children (Scotland) Act 1995;"; and

(d) for the definition of "supervision requirement" substitute—

""supervision requirement" has the meaning given by section 70(1) of the said Act of 1995;".

Criminal Justice (Scotland) Act 1980 (c. 62)

29.—(1) The Criminal Justice (Scotland) Act 1980 shall be amended in accordance with this paragraph.

(2) In section 3 (right to have someone informed when arrested or detained), in subsection (5)(b), for the words "actual custody" substitute "care".

(3) In Schedule 7, paragraph 21 (which confers jurisdiction on a sheriff for the purposes of certain applications under section 42 of the Social Work (Scotland) Act 1968) shall cease to have effect.

1968 c. 49.

Matrimonial Homes (Family Protection) (Scotland) Act 1981 (c. 59)

30. In section 22 of the Matrimonial Homes (Family Protection) (Scotland) Act 1981 (interpretation), in the definition of "child", for the word "accepted" substitute "treated".

Civil Jurisdiction and Judgments Act 1982 (c. 27)

31. In Schedule 9 to the Civil Jurisdiction and Judgments Act 1982 (excluded proceedings), after paragraph 2 insert—

"2A. Proceedings relating to parental responsibilities within the meaning of section 1(3) of the Children (Scotland) Act 1995 or parental rights within the meaning of section 2(4) of that Act.".

Health and Social Services and Social Security Adjudications Act 1983 (c. 41)

32. In Schedule 2 to the Health and Social Services and Social Security Adjudications Act 1983, paragraphs 4 to 6 and 8 (which amend provisions of the Social Work (Scotland) Act 1968 repealed by this Act) shall cease to have effect.

Mental Health (Scotland) Act 1984 (c. 36)

33.—(1) The Mental Health (Scotland) Act 1984 shall be amended in accordance with this paragraph.

(2) In section 10(1) (application of provisions relating to certain patients suffering from mental disorder)—

(a) in paragraph (a), sub-paragraph (i), and the word "or" immediately following that sub-paragraph, shall cease to have effect; and

(b) after paragraph (a) insert—

"(aa) a child or young person in relation to whom parental rights and responsibilities have been transferred to a local authority by virtue of section 86(1) of the Children (Scotland) Act 1995;".

(3) In section 54 (local authority to be deemed nearest relative of certain children and young persons), for paragraph (a) substitute—

"(a) the parental rights and responsibilities in relation to a patient who is a child or young person have been transferred to a local authority by virtue of section 86(1) of the Children (Scotland) Act 1995;".

(4) In section 55 (nearest relative of child under guardianship etc.)—

(a) for subsection (1) substitute—

"(1) Where—

(a) a guardian has been appointed for a child who has not attained the age of eighteen years; or

(b) there is in force a residence order, or a custody order, granted by a court in the United Kingdom, or an analogous order granted by a court outwith the United Kingdom (being an order which is entitled to recognition in Scotland), identifying a person as the person with whom a child under the age of sixteen years is to live,

that guardian or person shall, to the exclusion of any other person, be deemed to be the child's nearest relative.";

(b) for subsection (3) substitute—

"(3) In this section "guardian" does not include a guardian under this Part of this Act or, in relation to a child, a guardian whose appointment takes effect under section 7, or on an order under section 11(1), of the Children (Scotland) Act 1995 where there is a parent who has parental responsibilities and parental rights in relation to the child."; and

(c) subsection (4) shall cease to have effect.

Child Abduction Act 1984 (c. 37)

34. In section 6 of the Child Abduction Act 1984 (offence in Scotland of person connected with a child taking or sending that child out of United Kingdom)—

(a) in subsection (1)(a)(i), after the word "person" insert "or naming any person as the person with whom the child is to live";

(b) in subsection (2)(b), after the words "to him" insert "or naming him as the person with whom the child is to live"; and

(c) in subsection (3)(a)(i)(b), for the word "(whether" substitute "or who is named as the person with whom the child is to live (whether the award is made, or the person so named is named".

Foster Children (Scotland) Act 1984 (c. 56)

35.—(1) The Foster Children (Scotland) Act 1984 shall be amended in accordance with this paragraph.

(2) In section 2 (exceptions to definition of "foster child")—

(a) in subsection (1), for the words "in the care of a local authority or a voluntary organisation" substitute "being looked after by a local authority";

(b) in subsection (3), the words "within the meaning of the Social Work (Scotland) Act 1968" shall cease to have effect;

(c) in subsection (5), the words "; or (b) while he is a protected child within the meaning of section 32 of the said Act of 1978" shall cease to have effect; and

(d) after subsection (5) add—

"(6) The reference in subsection (1) above to a child being looked after by a local authority shall be construed as if it were a reference to which section 17(6) of the Children (Scotland) Act 1995 applies.".

(3) In section 3(4) (saving for Social Work (Scotland) Act 1968), for the words "the Social Work (Scotland) Act 1968" substitute "Part II of the Children (Scotland) Act 1995".

(4) In section 7(1) (persons disqualified from keeping foster children)—

(a) in paragraph (b), after the word "1968" insert "or under section 70 of the Children (Scotland) Act 1995"; and

(b) after paragraph (d) insert—

"(dd) his parental rights and parental responsibilities (within the meaning of the Children (Scotland) Act 1995) have been transferred, by an order under section 86(1) of that Act, to a local authority;".

(5) In section 12 (removal of foster children on complaint of local authority), for subsection (5) substitute—

"(5) For the purposes of section 25 of the Children (Scotland) Act 1995 (and for the reason mentioned in subsection (1)(c) of that section) a child removed under this section shall be regarded as requiring accommodation.".

(6) In section 13 (which makes provision as to the effect of a refusal to allow a visit to a foster child or to allow premises to be inspected), for the words from "sections" to the end substitute "section 55 of the Children (Scotland) Act 1995 (child assessment orders) as giving the local authority reasonable cause for the suspicion mentioned in subsection (1)(a) of that section.".

(7) In section 21(1) (interpretation)—

(a) in the definition of "residential establishment", after the word "1968" insert "or of Part II of the Children (Scotland) Act 1995"; and

(b) for the definition of "supervision requirement", substitute—

""supervision requirement" has the meaning given by section 70(1) of the Children (Scotland) Act 1995;".

Family Law (Scotland) Act 1985 (c. 37)

36. In section 2 of the Family Law (Scotland) Act 1985 (actions for aliment)—

(a) in subsection (2), for paragraph (c) substitute—

"(c) concerning parental responsibilities or parental rights (within the meaning of sections 1(3) and 2(4) respectively of the Children (Scotland) Act 1995) or guardianship in relation to children;"; and

(b) in subsection (4)(c), for sub-paragraph (iii) substitute—

"(iii) a person with whom the child lives or who is seeking a residence order (within the meaning of section 11(2)(c) of the Children (Scotland) Act 1995) in respect of the child.".

Child Abduction and Custody Act 1985 (c. 60)

37.—(1) The Child Abduction and Custody Act 1985 shall be amended in accordance with this paragraph.

(2) In section 9 (suspension of court's powers in cases of wrongful removal), for paragraph (d) substitute—

"(d) making, varying or discharging an order under section 86 of the Children (Scotland) Act 1995;".

(3) In section 20 (further provision as regards suspension of court's powers)—

(a) for paragraph (d) substitute—

"(d) in the case of proceedings for, or for the variation or discharge of, a parental responsibilities order under section 86 of the Children (Scotland) Act 1995, make, vary or discharge any such order;"; and

(b) in subsection (5), for the words "within the meaning of Part III of the Social Work (Scotland) Act 1968" substitute "(as defined in section 93(1) of the Children (Scotland) Act 1995)".

(4) In section 25 (termination of existing custody orders etc.), subsection (6) shall cease to have effect.

(5) In section 27(4) (interpretation), after the word "Wales" insert "or Scotland".

(6) In Schedule 3 (custody orders)—

(a) in paragraph 5—

(i) for the words "custody, care or control of a child or" substitute "residence, custody, care or control of a child or contact with, or";

(ii) in sub-paragraph (iii), for the words "tutory or curatory" substitute "guardianship";

(iii) in sub-paragraph (iv), for the words "16(8), 16A(3) or 18(3) of the Social Work (Scotland) Act 1968" substitute "86 of the Children (Scotland) Act 1995"; and

(iv) for sub-paragraph (v), substitute—

"(v) an order made, or warrant or authorisation granted, under or by virtue of Chapter 2 or 3 of Part II of the Children (Scotland) Act 1995 to remove the child to a place of safety or to secure accommodation, to keep him at such a place or in such accommodation, or to prevent his removal from a place where he is being accommodated (or an order varying or discharging any order, warrant or authorisation so made or granted);";

(b) for paragraph 6 substitute—

"6. A supervision requirement made by a children's hearing under section 70 of the Children (Scotland) Act 1995 (whether or not continued under section 73 of that Act) or made by the sheriff under section 51(5)(c)(iii) of that Act and any order made by a court in England and Wales or in Northern Ireland if it is an order which, by virtue of section 33(1) of that Act, has effect as if it were such a supervision requirement."; and

(c) paragraph 7 shall cease to have effect.

Law Reform (Parent and Child) (Scotland) Act 1986 (c. 9)

38.—(1) The Law Reform (Parent and Child) (Scotland) Act 1986 shall be amended in accordance with this paragraph.

(2) In section 1 (legal equality of children), for subsection (3) substitute—

"(3) Subsection (1) above is subject to subsection (4) below, to section 9(1) of this Act and to section 3(1)(b) of the Children (Scotland) Act 1995 (parental responsibilities and parental rights of natural father).".

(3) In section 6(2) (consent to taking of sample of blood), for the words from "guardian" to "custody or" substitute "any person having parental responsibilities (within the meaning of section 1(3) of the Children (Scotland) Act 1995) in relation to him or having".

Disabled Persons (Services, Consultation and Representation) Act 1986 (c. 33)

39.—(1) The Disabled Persons (Services, Consultation and Representation) Act 1986 shall be amended in accordance with this paragraph.

(2) In section 1(3) (regulations with respect to appointment of authorised representatives of disabled persons)—

(a) in paragraph (a), for the words from the beginning to "appoint" substitute—

"may provide for—

(i) any person who has parental responsibilities in relation to a disabled person under the age of sixteen ("parental responsibilities" having the meaning given by section 1(3) of the Children (Scotland) Act 1995); or

(ii) any other person who is entitled to act as the disabled person's legal representative (as defined in section 15(5) of the Children (Scotland) Act 1995),

to appoint"; and

(b) in paragraph (b), for the words "in the care of" substitute "looked after by".

(3) In section 2 (rights of certain authorised representatives of disabled persons)—

(a) in subsection (3)(a), for the words "the words "the parent or guardian of" shall be inserted after the words "if so requested by";" substitute "for the words "by the disabled person" there shall be substituted the words "by any person appointed by virtue of regulations made under section 1(3)(a)(i) or (ii) of this Act";"; and

(b) in subsection (5), after paragraph (bb) insert—

"(bc) in Scotland, in accommodation provided by or on behalf of a local authority under Chapter 1 of Part II of the Children (Scotland) Act 1995, or".

(4) In section 13(8)(b) (limitation on requirement for assessment of needs)—

(a) for the words "his parent" substitute "any person having parental responsibilities in relation to him"; and

(b) after the word "request" insert "("parental responsibilities" having the meaning given in section 1(3) of the Children (Scotland) Act 1995)".

(5) In section 16 (interpretation)—

(a) in the definition of "disabled person", for paragraph (b) substitute—

"(b) in relation to Scotland, means—

(i) in the case of a person aged eighteen or over, one chronically sick or disabled or one suffering from mental disorder (being, in either case, a relevant person for the purposes of section 12 of the Social Work (Scotland) Act 1968); and

(ii) in any other case, a disabled child ("disabled child" being construed in accordance with Chapter 1 of Part II of the Children (Scotland) Act 1995);";

(b) in the definition of "guardian", paragraph (b) shall cease to have effect;

(c) in the definition of "the welfare enactments", in paragraph (b), for the words "and sections 7 and 8 of the 1984 Act", substitute ", sections 7 and 8 of the 1984 Act and Chapter 1 of Part II of the Children (Scotland) Act 1995"; and

(d) the existing provisions as so amended shall be subsection (1) of the section and at the end of the section there shall be added—

"(2A) In this Act as it applies in relation to Scotland, any reference to a child who is looked after by a local authority shall be construed in accordance with section 17(6) of the Children (Scotland) Act 1995.".

Legal Aid (Scotland) Act 1986 (c. 47)

40. In section 41 of the Legal Aid (Scotland) Act 1986 (interpretation)—

(a) in the definition of "legal aid", for the words "Part III of the Social Work (Scotland Act 1968" substitute "Chapter 2 or Chapter 3 of Part II of the Children (Scotland) Act 1995; and

(b) in the definition of "person", the existing words from "does" to the end shall be paragraph (a) and after that paragraph there shall be added—
"; and

(b) includes a person under the age of sixteen years.".

Family Law Act 1986 (c. 55)

41.—(1) The Family Law Act 1986 shall be amended in accordance with this paragraph.

(2) In section 1(1)(b) (meaning of "custody order")—

(a) for the words "custody, care or control of a child" substitute "residence, custody, care or control of a child, contact with or"; and

(b) in sub-paragraph (iv), for the words "for the custody of" substitute "giving parental responsibilities and parental rights in relation to".

(3) In section 13 (jurisdiction ancillary to matrimonial proceedings)—

(a) in subsection (2), for the words "under section 9(1) of the Matrimonial Proceedings (Children) Act 1958" substitute "in those proceedings"; and

(b) in subsection (4), for the words "under section 9(1) of the Matrimonial Proceedings (Children) Act 1958" substitute "in matrimonial proceedings where the court has refused to grant the principal remedy sought in the proceedings".

(4) In section 15 (duration, variation and recall of orders)—

(a) in subsection (1)(b), for the words "for the custody of" substitute "relating to the parental responsibilities or parental rights in relation to"; and

(b) in subsection (4), for the words from the beginning to "above" substitute "Where, by virtue of subsection (1) above, a child is to live with a different person".

(5) In section 17 (orders for delivery of child)—

(a) in subsection (3), for the words from "is the child" to "other party" substitute ", although not a child of both parties to the marriage, is a child of the family of those parties"; and

(b) at the end of the section add—

"(4) In subsection (3) above, "child of the family" means any child who has been treated by both parties as a child of their family, except a child who has been placed with those parties as foster parents by a local authority or a voluntary organisation.".

(6) For section 26 (recognition: special Scottish rule), substitute—

"Recognition: special Scottish rule.　　26. An order relating to parental responsibilities or parental rights in relation to a child which is made outside the United Kingdom shall be recognised in Scotland if the order was made in the country where the child was habitually resident.".

(7) In section 33(3) (power to order disclosure of child's whereabouts), for the words "for the custody of" substitute "relating to parental responsibilities or parental rights in relation to".

(8) In section 35(3) (power to restrict removal of child from jurisdiction), for the words "whose custody" substitute "whose care".

(9) In section 42 (interpretation)—

(a) in subsection (1), before the definition of "part of the United Kingdom" insert—

""parental responsibilities" and "parental rights" have the meanings respectively given by sections 1(3) and 2(4) of the Children (Scotland) Act 1995;"; and

(b) in subsection (4)(b), for the words from "of one of the parties" to the end substitute "who has been treated by both parties as a child of their family, except a child who has been placed with those parties as foster parents by a local authority or a voluntary organisation;".

Housing (Scotland) Act 1987 (c. 26)

42. In section 61 of the Housing (Scotland) Act 1987 (exemption from secure tenant's right to purchase)—

(a) in subsection (4)(f)(iii), for the words "have left the care of" substitute "as children have been looked after by"; and

(b) after subsection (4) add—

"(4A) The reference in subsection (4)(f)(iii) above to children looked after by a local authority shall be construed in accordance with section 17(6) of the Children (Scotland) Act 1995.".

Criminal Justice (Scotland) Act 1987 (c. 41)

43. In section 49(4)(b) of the Criminal Justice (Scotland) Act 1987 (right to have someone informed when detained), for the words "actual custody" substitute "care".

Civil Evidence (Scotland) Act 1988 (c. 32)

44. In paragraph (a) of the definition of "civil proceedings" in section 9 of the Civil Evidence (Scotland) Act 1988 (interpretation)—

(a) the words "under section 42 of the Social Work (Scotland) Act 1968" shall cease to have effect;

(b) after the word "application" where it first occurs insert "under section 65(7) or (9) of the Children (Scotland) Act 1995";

(c) after the word "established," insert "or of an application for a review of such a finding under section 85 of that Act";

(d) after the word "application" where it occurs for the second time insert "or, as the case may be, the review"; and

(e) for the words "32(2)(g)" substitute "52(2)(i)".

Court of Session Act 1988 (c. 36)

45. In section 5 of the Court of Session Act 1988 (power to regulate procedure etc. by act of sederunt), after paragraph (e) insert—

"(ee) to permit a person who is not an advocate or solicitor and is not represented by an advocate or solicitor to transmit, whether orally or in writing, the views of a child to the Court for the purposes of any enactment which makes provision (however expressed) for the Court to have regard to those views;".

School Boards (Scotland) Act 1988 (c. 47)

46. In section 22(2) of the School Boards (Scotland) Act 1988 (interpretation), in the definition of "parent", for the word "custody" substitute "parental responsibilities (within the meaning of section 1(3) of the Children (Scotland) Act 1995) in relation to him or who has care".

Self-Governing Schools etc. (Scotland) Act 1989 (c. 39)

47. In section 80(1) of the Self-Governing Schools etc. (Scotland) Act 1989 (interpretation), in the definition of "parent", for the words "the actual custody" substitute "parental responsibilities (within the meaning of section 1(3) of the Children (Scotland) Act 1995) in relation to him or has care".

Children Act 1989 (c. 41)

48.—(1) The Children Act 1989 shall be amended in accordance with this paragraph.

(2) In section 31(7)(b)(iii) (restriction on applications for care and supervision orders), for the words "the Social Work (Scotland) Act 1968" substitute "Part II of the Children (Scotland) Act 1995".

(3) In section 51(7) (enactments which do not apply where a child is granted refuge), for paragraph (b) substitute—

"(b) sections 82 (recovery of certain fugitive children) and 83 (harbouring) of the Children (Scotland) Act 1995, so far as they apply in relation to anything done in England and Wales;".

(4) In section 79(e) (application of Part X to Scotland), for the words from "in whom" to "vested" substitute "having parental responsibilities (within the meaning of section 1(3) of the Children (Scotland) Act 1995) relating to the child".

(5) In Schedule 8 (privately fostered children), in paragraph 3(b), for the words "the Social Work (Scotland) Act 1968" substitute "Part II of the Children (Scotland) Act 1995".

Local Government and Housing Act 1989 (c. 42)

49.—(1) The Local Government and Housing Act 1989 shall be amended in accordance with this paragraph.

(2) In section 14(5) (restriction of effect of provisions of that section in relation to certain committees), for paragraph (d) substitute—

"(d) a Children's Panel Advisory Committee formed under paragraph 3, or a joint advisory committee formed under paragraph 8, of Schedule 1 to the Children (Scotland) Act 1995;".

Access to Health Records Act 1990 (c. 23)

50.—(1) The Access to Health Records Act 1990 shall be amended in accordance with this paragraph.

(2) In section 3(1) (right of access to health records), for paragraphs (c) and (d) substitute—

"(cc) where the patient is a child, a person having parental responsibility for him;".

(3) In section 4 (cases where right of access may be wholly excluded)—

(a) in subsection (1), for paragraphs (a) and (b) substitute "the patient is a child"; and

(b) in subsection (2), for the words "(1)(c) or (d)" substitute "(1)(cc)".

(4) In section 5(3) (access to records not to be given where record compiled on basis that access would not be available to particular applicant), for the words "(1)(c), (d), (e) or (f)" substitute "(1)(cc), (e) or (f)".

(5) In section 11 (interpretation), for the definition of "parental responsibility" substitute—

""parental responsibility", in the application of this Act—

(a) to England and Wales, has the same meaning as in the Children Act 1989; and   1989 c. 41.

(b) to Scotland, shall be construed as a reference to "parental responsibilities" within the meaning given by section 1(3) of the Children (Scotland) Act 1995.".

Horses (Protective Headgear for Young Riders) Act 1990 (c. 25)

51. In section 1(2)(a)(ii) (application), of the Horses (Protective Headgear for Young Riders) Act 1990, for the word "custody" substitute "parental responsibilities (within the meaning given by section 1(3) of the Children (Scotland) Act 1995) in relation to, or has".

Child Support Act 1991 (c. 48)

52.—(1) The Child Support Act 1991 shall be amended in accordance with this paragraph.

(2) In section 3(4)(d) (interpretation), for the words from "having" to the end substitute "with whom a child is to live by virtue of a residence order under section 11 of the Children (Scotland) Act 1995.".

(3) In section 5(1) (supplemental provisions as respects child support maintenance), the words "(or, in Scotland, parental rights over)", in both places where they occur, shall cease to have effect.

(4) In section 54 (interpretation)—

(a) for the definition of "parental responsibility" substitute—

""parental responsibility", in the application of this Act—

(a) to England and Wales, has the same meaning as in the Children Act 1989; and

(b) to Scotland, shall be construed as a reference to "parental responsibilities" within the meaning given by section 1(3) of the Children (Scotland) Act 1995;"; and

(b) the definition of "parental rights" shall cease to have effect.

Age of Legal Capacity (Scotland) Act 1991 (c. 50)

53.—(1) The Age of Legal Capacity (Scotland) Act 1991 shall be amended in accordance with this paragraph.

(2) In section 1(3) (age of legal capacity)—

(a) in sub-paragraph (i) of paragraph (f), for the words "who has no guardian or whose guardian" substitute "in relation to whom there is no person entitled to act as his legal representative (within the meaning of Part I of the Children (Scotland) Act 1995), or where there is such a person"; and

(b) in paragraph (g), for sub-paragraphs (i) and (ii) substitute "exercising parental responsibilities and parental rights (within the meaning of sections 1(3) and 2(4) respectively of the Children (Scotland) Act 1995) in relation to any child of his.".

(3) In section 2 (exceptions to the general rule), after subsection (4) insert—

"(4A) A person under the age of sixteen years shall have legal capacity to instruct a solicitor, in connection with any civil matter, where that person has a general understanding of what it means to do so; and without prejudice to the generality of this subsection a person twelve years of age or more shall be presumed to be of sufficient age and maturity to have such understanding.

(4B) A person who by virtue of subsection (4A) above has legal capacity to instruct a solicitor shall also have legal capacity to sue, or to defend, in any civil proceedings.

(4C) Subsections (4A) and (4B) above are without prejudice to any question of legal capacity arising in connection with any criminal matter.".

(4) In section 5(1) (construction of references to "tutor")—

(a) the words "or tutory" shall cease to have effect; and

(b) for the words from "the guardian", where they first appear, to the end substitute "a person entitled to act as a child's legal representative (within the meaning of Part I of the Children (Scotland) Act 1995), and any reference to the tutory of such a child shall be construed as a reference to the entitlement to act as a child's legal representative enjoyed by a person by, under or by virtue of the said Part I.".

(5) In section 5(2) (restriction on appointment of guardian to person under sixteen), for the words from "section 3" to the end substitute "section 7 of the Children (Scotland) Act 1995.".

Armed Forces Act 1991 (c. 62)

54.—(1) The Armed Forces Act 1991 shall be amended in accordance with this paragraph.

(2) In paragraph (f) of section 17(4) (persons to whom notice of an application for an assessment order must be given)—

(a) after the word "order" insert "—

(i)"; and

(b) at the end insert "; or

(ii) under section 88 of the Children (Scotland) Act 1995".

(3) In paragraph (f) of section 18(7) (persons who may apply for variation etc. of assessment order)—

(a) after the word "order" insert "—

(i)"; and

(b) at the end insert "; or

(ii) under section 88 of the Children (Scotland) Act 1995".

(4) In section 21(4) (which makes provision in relation to a child returned to the United Kingdom under a protection order under that Act) for the words "Social Work (Scotland) Act 1968" substitute "Children (Scotland) Act 1995".   1968 c. 49.

(5) In section 23(1) (interpretation)—

(a) in the definition of "contact order"—

(i) after the word "meaning" insert "—

(a) except in relation to an order made in Scotland,"; and

(ii) at the end, add "; and

(b) in relation to an order there made, given by section 11(2)(d) of the Children (Scotland) Act 1995."; and

(b) in the definition of "parental responsibility"—

(i) after the word "responsibility"" insert "—

(a) except in relation to Scotland,"; and

(ii) at the end add "; and

(b) in relation to Scotland, shall be construed as a reference to "parental responsibilities" within the meaning given by section 1(3) of the Children (Scotland) Act 1995;".

Tribunals and Inquiries Act 1992 (c. 53)

55. In paragraph 61 in column 2 of Schedule 1 to the Tribunals and Inquiries Act 1992 (which specifies certain tribunals in relation to social work in Scotland)—

(a) in sub-paragraph (a), for the words "Social Work (Scotland) Act 1968 (c.49)" substitute "Children (Scotland) Act 1995 (c.36)"; and

(b) in sub-paragraph (b), for the words "that Act" substitute "the Social Work (Scotland) Act 1968 (c.49)".

Prisoners and Criminal Proceedings (Scotland) Act 1993 (c. 9)

56.—(1) The Prisoners and Criminal Proceedings (Scotland) Act 1993 shall be amended in accordance with this paragraph.

(2) In paragraph 8 of Schedule 3 (which provides for the definition of certain expressions in relation to the admission of documentary evidence in criminal proceedings), in the definition of "criminal proceedings"—

(a) the words "under section 42 of the Social Work (Scotland) Act 1968" shall cease to have effect;

(b) after the word "application" where it appears for the first time insert "under section 65(7) or (9) of the Children (Scotland) Act 1995";

(c) after the word "established" insert "or for a review of such a finding under section 85 of that Act"; and

(d) after the word "application", where it appears for the second time, insert "or, as the case may be, the review".

(3) In paragraph 1 of Schedule 6 (which provides for the definition of certain expressions in relation to transitional provisions), in the definition of "existing child detainee", for the words "section 30 of the Social Work (Scotland) Act 1968" substitute "section 93(2)(b) of the Children (Scotland) Act 1995".

Local Government etc. (Scotland) Act 1994 (c. 39)

57.—(1) The Local Government etc. (Scotland) Act 1994 shall be amended in accordance with this paragraph.

(2) In section 128 (establishment of Scottish Children's Reporter Administration)—

(a) in subsection (3), for the words from "the 1968 Act" to the end substitute "the Children (Scotland) Act 1995 and any other enactment conferring functions upon him"; and

(b) in subsection (8), for the words from "the 1968 Act" to the end substitute "the Children (Scotland) Act 1995 and any other enactment conferring functions upon him".

(3) In section 130 (annual reports by Principal Reporter) in sub-paragraph (i) of paragraph (a) of subsection (1), for the words "the 1968 Act and the Criminal Procedure (Scotland) Act 1975" substitute "the Children (Scotland) Act 1995 and any other enactment (except this Act) conferring functions upon him".

(4) In section 132 (duty of Administration to provide accommodation for children's hearings), for the words "section 34 of the 1968 Act" substitute "section 39 of the Children (Scotland) Act 1995".

Children (Northern Ireland) Order 1995 (SI 1995/755 (N.I.2))

58. In Article 70(7) of the Children (Northern Ireland) Order 1995 (enactments not to apply where child given refuge), in sub-paragraph (c), for the words "section 71 of the Social Work (Scotland) Act 1968" substitute "section 83 of the Children (Scotland) Act 1995".

Civil Evidence (Family Mediation)(Scotland) Act 1995 (c. 6)

59. In section 2 of the Civil Evidence (Family Mediation) (Scotland) Act 1995 (which provides for exceptions to the general inadmissibility of evidence concerning family mediation), in paragraph (d)(ii)—

(a) for the words "Part III of the Social Work (Scotland) Act 1968" substitute "Chapter 2 or 3 of Part II of the Children (Scotland) Act 1995"; and

(b) after the word "hearing" insert—

", before a sheriff or before a justice of the peace;

(iia) on any appeal arising from such proceedings as are mentioned in sub-paragraph (ii) above".

Criminal Justice (Scotland) Act 1995 (c. 20)

60. In section 20 of the Criminal Justice (Scotland) Act 1995 (construction of sections relating to the admissibility of certain evidence)—

(a) in subsection (3), in the definition of "criminal proceedings"—

(i) for the words from "under" to "application", where it appears for the first time, substitute "of an application made under Chapter 3 of Part II of the Children (Scotland) Act 1995"; and

(ii) after the word "child" insert "or for a review of such a finding"; and

(b) in subsection (5), after the words "1968" insert "or by virtue of Chapter 3 of Part II of the Children (Scotland) Act 1995".

SCHEDULE 5

REPEALS

Section 105(5).

Chapter	Short title	Extent of repeal
8 & 9 Vict. c.19.	Lands Clauses Consolidation (Scotland) Act 1845.	In section 7, the words "persons under legal disability by reason of nonage" in each place where they occur. In section 67, the words "persons under legal disability by reason of nonage". In section 69, the words "persons under legal disability by reason of nonage".
12 & 13 Vict. c.51.	Judicial Factors Act 1849.	In section 1, the words from "the word "Guardian"" to "years;". Section 25(2) In section 27, the words "guardians and". In section 31, the word "guardian,". In section 32, the word "guardian,". In section 33, the words "guardians or". In section 34, in both places where it occurs, the word "guardian,". In section 36, the word "guardianships,". In section 37, the word "guardian," In section 40, the word "guardians," in both places where it occurs.

Chapter	Short title	Extent of repeal
27 & 28 Vict. c.114.	Improvement of Land Act 1864.	In section 18, the words from "nor shall they" to the end. In section 21, the words from "or if the landowner" to "minors"; and the words "or circumstance" in both places where they occur.
43 & 44 Vict. c.4.	Judicial Factors (Scotland) Act 1880.	In section 3, in the definition of "judicial factor", the words from "and" to "required".
7 Edw.7 c.51.	Sheriff Courts (Scotland) Act 1907.	Section 5(2C). Section 38C.
11 & 12 Geo.5 c.58.	Trusts (Scotland) Act 1921.	In section 2, in the definition of "trustee", the words from "guardian" to "years)".
1 Edw.8 & 1 Geo.6 c.37.	Children and Young Persons (Scotland) Act 1937.	In section 27, the first paragraph.
1 & 2 Geo.6 c.73.	Nursing Homes Registration (Scotland) Act 1938.	In section 4(1)(b)(iii), the words "custody or".
14 & 15 Geo.6 c.65.	Reserve and Auxiliary Forces (Protection of Civil Interests) Act 1951.	In section 8(1)(d), the words from "or any order" to the end.
6 & 7 Eliz.2 c.40.	Matrimonial Proceedings (Children) Act 1958.	Sections 8 to 10. Section 12.
1965 c.49.	Registration of Births, Deaths and Marriages (Scotland) Act 1965.	In section 43, in subsection (3) the words from "In this" to the end; and subsection (10).
1968 c.49.	Social Work (Scotland) Act 1968.	In section 5(1B), before paragraph (o), the word "and". In section 5B(5), the words from "and" at the end of the definition of child to the end of the subsection. Section 6(1)(b)(ii). Sections 15 to 26. Part III, except section 31(1) and (3). Part V. Section 88. In section 90(1), the words "(other than orders under sections 52 and 58 and Part V of this Act)". In section 94(1), the definition of "children's panel" and of "children's hearing"; the definitions

Chapter	Short title	Extent of repeal
		of "compulsory measures of care", "guardian" and "place of safety"; in the definition of "prescribed", paragraph (b); and the definition of "school age". In section 97, in subsection (1), the words "section 44(1) (except head (b)) and (1A)", "section 58" and "Part V"; and subsections (2) and (3).
1969 c.54.	Children and Young Persons Act 1969.	In Schedule 5, paragraphs 57 and 65(1).
1972 c.18.	Maintenance Orders (Reciprocal Enforcement) Act 1972.	Section 4(3).
1972 c.24.	Social Work (Scotland) Act 1972.	The whole Act.
1973 c.29.	Guardianship Act 1973.	The whole Act.
1973 c.65.	Local Government (Scotland) Act 1973.	In Schedule 25, paragraph 41. In Schedule 27, paragraphs 185 and 187.
1974 c.53.	Rehabilitation of Offenders Act 1974.	Section 5(10A). In section 7(2), paragraph (e); and the words from "In the application" to the end.
1975 c.21.	Criminal Procedure (Scotland) Act 1975.	Section 14. In section 168(c), the word "female". In section 177, the words "provided by a local authority under Part IV of the Social Work (Scotland) Act 1968". In section 296, in subsection (3), the words from "and the child" to the end; and subsection (4). Section 323. In section 364(c), the word "female". In section 378, the words "provided by a local authority under Part IV of the Social Work (Scotland) Act 1968". In section 413, in subsection (3), the definitions of "care" and of "the 1968 Act"; in subsection (4), the words "within the meaning of the 1968 Act"; in subsection (5), the words "(within the

Chapter	Short title	Extent of repeal
		meaning of the 1968 Act)"; and in subsection (6A), the words "within the meaning of the 1968 Act".
		In Schedule 9, paragraphs 43 and 44.
1975 c.72.	Children Act 1975.	Sections 47 to 49.
		Section 53.
		Sections 73 to 84.
		Sections 99 and 100.
		Section 102.
		Section 103.
		Section 105.
		Section 107, except the definitions, in subsection (1), of "adoption society", "child" and "voluntary organisation".
		In Schedule 3, paragraphs 52 to 57.
1978 c.28.	Adoption (Scotland) Act 1978.	In section 1(2), paragraph (a).
		In section 2, paragraph (d).
		In section 3(3)(a), the words "including in particular its ability to make provision for children who are free for adoption".
		Section 8.
		In section 12, in subsection (3)(b), the words "or by"; and in subsection (4) the word "—(a)" and paragraph (b).
		In section 14(1), the words from "Subject" to "certain cases)".
		In section 15, in subsection (1), the words from "Subject" to "certain cases)"; and in subsection (3), the word "natural" wherever it occurs.
		In section 16, subsection (5).
		Section 26.
		In section 28(5), the words "or of a voluntary organisation" and "or the organisation".
		Sections 32 to 37.
		In section 51, subsections (6)(a) and (7) to (11).
		In section 60(3), the words "or 51(9)".
		In section 65(1), in the definition of "guardian", paragraph (b); and in the definition of "local

Chapter	Short title	Extent of repeal
		authority", the words ", 35(1)". In Schedule 3, paragraphs 13, 14 and 15.
1980 c.44.	Education (Scotland) Act 1980.	Section 44(1). In section 65B(6), paragraph (a). In section 135(1), the definition of "reporter of the appropriate local authority".
1980 c.62.	Criminal Justice (Scotland) Act 1980.	In Schedule 7, paragraph 21.
1983 c.33.	Solvent Abuse (Scotland) Act 1983.	The whole Act.
1983 c.41.	Health and Social Services and Social Security Adjudications Act 1983.	Section 7. Section 8(1) and (4). In Schedule 2, paragraphs 4 to 6 and 8.
1984 c.15.	Law Reform (Husband and Wife) (Scotland) Act 1984.	Section 3(2).
1984 c.36.	Mental Health (Scotland) Act 1984.	In section 10(1)(a), sub-paragraph (i); and the word "or" immediately following that sub-paragraph. Section 55(4).
1984 c.56.	Foster Children (Scotland) Act 1984.	In section 2, in subsection (3), the words "within the meaning of the Social Work (Scotland) Act 1968"; and in subsection (5), the words "; or (b) while he is a protected child within the meaning of section 32 of the said Act of 1978.".
1985 c.37.	Family Law (Scotland) Act 1985.	In section 21, the words from "or an order" to "child".
1985 c.60.	Child Abduction and Custody Act 1985.	In section 25, subsection (6). In Schedule 3, paragraph 7.
1986 c.9.	Law Reform (Parent and Child) (Scotland) Act 1986.	Sections 2 to 4. In section 8, the definitions of "child" and "parental rights". In Schedule 1, paragraph 3.
1986 c.33.	Disabled Persons (Services, Consultation and Representation) Act 1986.	In section 16, in the definition of "guardian", paragraph (b).
1986 c.55.	Family Law Act 1986.	In section 15(4), the words from "under section" to "1973". In section 17, in subsection

Chapter	Short title	Extent of repeal
		(1), the words "Subject to subsection (2) below"; and subsection (2). In section 35(4)(c), the words "custody or".
1988 c.32.	Civil Evidence (Scotland) Act 1988.	In section 9, in the definition of "civil proceedings", in paragraph (a), the words "under section 42 of the Social Work (Scotland) Act 1968".
1988 c.36.	Court of Session Act 1988.	Section 20.
1989 c.41.	Children Act 1989.	In Schedule 13, paragraph 13.
1989 c.42.	Local Government and Housing Act 1989.	In Schedule 11, paragraph 15.
1991 c.48.	Child Support Act 1991.	In section 5(1), the words "(or, in Scotland, parental rights over)" in both places where they occur. In section 54, the definition of "parental rights".
1991 c.50.	Age of Legal Capacity (Scotland) Act 1991.	In section 5(1), the words "or tutory". In section 9, the definition of "parental rights". In Schedule 1, paragraphs 3 to 5 and 7 to 15.
1993 c.9.	Prisoners and Criminal Proceedings (Scotland) Act 1993.	In paragraph 8 of Schedule 3, in the definition of "criminal proceedings", the words "under section 42 of the Social Work (Scotland) Act 1968".
1993 c.35.	Education Act 1993.	In Schedule 19, paragraph 36.
1994 c.39.	Local Government etc. (Scotland) Act 1994.	Section 139. In Schedule 13, paragraphs 76(6) and (10) to (25); 92(14)(b)(iii); 100(6)(b)(iv); 103; and 161(7)(c).

PRINTED IN THE UNITED KINGDOM BY MIKE LYNN
Controller and Chief Executive of Her Majesty's Stationery Office
and Queen's Printer of Acts of Parliament